Books by Erin McHugh:

WHO?

WHAT?

WHERE?

WHEN?

WHY?

WHEN?

ERIN McHUGH

Sterling Publishing Co., Inc.
New York

Library of Congress Cataloging-in-Publication Data Available

10 9 8 7 6 5 4 3 2 1

Published by Sterling Publishing Co., Inc.
387 Park Avenue South, New York, NY 10016
© 2005 by Erin McHugh
Distributed in Canada by Sterling Publishing
℅ Canadian Manda Group, 165 Dufferin Street
Toronto, Ontario, Canada M6K 3H6
Distributed in Great Britain by Chrysalis Books Group PLC
The Chrysalis Building, Bramley Road, London W10 6SP, England
Distributed in Australia by Capricorn Link (Australia) Pty. Ltd.
P.O. Box 704, Windsor, NSW 2756, Australia

Sterling ISBN 1-4027-2571-X

For information about custom editions, special sales, premium and
corporate purchases, please contact Sterling Special Sales
Department at 800-805-5489 or specialsales@sterlingpub.com.

WHEN?

COME AND GET IT!
American Cuisine Changes Forever

What do you do with ten railroad cars of turkey? That's exactly what the management of the C. F. Swanson Company wondered back in 1953. They were stuck with too much meat (520,000 pounds of it) after Thanksgiving, and it was riding back and forth across the country in boxcars that would refrigerate only when riding the rails. The mandate to their employees: Find a home for the poultry. Salesman Gerry Thomas did just that, combining the concept of airline table trays and the shape of America's newest fad, the television. In went the frozen traveling turkey, accompanied by cornbread dressing with gravy, sweet potatoes, and buttered peas. The TV dinner was born.

The genius part of the frozen dinner, of course, was that each item in the tray was blanched at a different rate, so that when the dinner was cooked at home, the entire meal was ready at the same time. What Swanson didn't expect was that by calling the product a TV dinner, they would actually begin to change how—and where—American families gathered for their nightly meal. The first TV dinners cost ninety-eight cents, and a year later, Americans bought more than 10 million of them.

HELLO?

The SS *Great Eastern* laid the first successful transatlantic telegraph cable, 1,852 miles in length, between Valentia Island, Ireland, and Newfoundland, between July 13 and September 18, 1866.

WEATHER WATCH

August 1860–July 1861	Greatest twelve-month rainfall, in Cherrapunji, India: 1,042 inches
September 13, 1992	Highest temperature, in El Azizia, Libya: 136°F
July 21, 1983	Lowest temperature, in Vostok, Antarctica: −129°F

A **monsoon** occurs when there is a greater annual temperature variation over a large area of land than over its neighboring ocean surfaces. Its seasonal shift of winds usually blows out of the southwest from April to October, and out of the northeast from October to April.

A **snowstorm** is considered a blizzard when, for a duration of three hours or more, there is extreme cold, winds are over thirty-five miles per hour, and enough snow either falls or blows to reduce visibility to a quarter mile or less.

A **flood** is temporary submersion, partial or complete, of ordinarily dry land by water or mud, typically caused by an overflow of waters, whether inland, tidal, or from any accumulated runoff from any source.

NO GRAY AREA

The Pentagon was built in the early 1940s with twice as many bathrooms as were necessary. At that time, the state of Virginia still had segregation laws requiring separate toilet facilities for blacks and whites.

WHY YOU FORGET WHEN YOU FORGET

Amnesia is a disturbance of the memory of information in long-term memory. Types of amnesia are:

Anterograde amnesia: Inability to remember ongoing events after the incidence of trauma or the onset of the disease that might have caused said amnesia.

Emotional/hysterical amnesia: Memory loss caused when psychologically traumatized; usually a temporary condition.

Lacunar amnesia: Memory loss in which one is unable to remember a specific event.

Korsakoff syndrome: Memory loss caused by chronic alcoholism.

Posthypnotic amnesia: Memory loss sustained when one has been in a hypnotic state; can include inability to recall events that occurred during hypnosis or information stored in long-term memory.

Retrograde amnesia: Inability to remember events that occurred before the incidence of trauma or the onset of the disease that caused the amnesia.

Transient global amnesia: Spontaneous memory loss that can last from minutes to several hours; usually seen when one is middle-aged or elderly.

◆

The worst FLOOD in history occurred in 1931 along the Yangtze River in China; drowning, starvation, and disease caused the deaths of 3.7 million people.

THE YEAR OF YOU

The Chinese lunar calendar is the oldest chronological record in history, dating from 2600 BCE. Each year in the calendar is associated with an animal, in a cycle of twelve. The Chinese believe that of the twelve calendrical animals, the animal that rules the year in which a person is born has a profound influence on that person's personality: "This is the animal that hides in your heart." Beware, though, the beginning of the Chinese year is variable, from mid-January to mid-February.

Animal	Characteristics	Years
Rat	Humorous, charming, honest, yet greedy	1924, 1936, 1948, 1960, 1972, 1984, 1996
Ox	Tenacious, a leader, yet obstinate	1925, 1937, 1949, 1961, 1973, 1985, 1997
Tiger	Independent, courageous, warmhearted, yet resistant to authority	1926, 1938, 1950, 1962, 1974, 1986, 1998
Rabbit	Happy, refined, virtuous, yet superficial	1927, 1939, 1951, 1963, 1975, 1987, 1999
Dragon	Magical, lucky, artistic, sometimes ferocious	1928, 1940, 1952, 1964, 1976, 1988, 2000
Snake	Wise, philosophical, calm, can be calculating	1929, 1941, 1953, 1965, 1977, 1989, 2001

Animal	Characteristics	Years
Horse	Popular, quick-witted, hardworking, can be obstinate	1930, 1942, 1954, 1966, 1978, 1990, 2002
Sheep	Unassuming, innately intelligent, altruistic, yet misanthropic	1931, 1943, 1955, 1967, 1979, 1991, 2003
Monkey	Talkative, inquisitive, tricky, and egotistical	1932, 1944, 1956, 1968, 1980, 1992, 2004
Rooster	Courageous, frank, born organizers, yet blunt	1933, 1945, 1957, 1969, 1981, 1993, 2005
Dog	Humanitarian, just, empathic, yet defensive	1934, 1946, 1958, 1970, 1982, 1994, 2006
Boar	Pure, honest, fun, and extravagant	1935, 1947, 1959, 1971, 1983, 1995, 2007

◆

GOING, GOING, GONE

There are two ways that a person may be declared legally and medically dead: when the heart stops beating, or when the brain stops functioning. The latter is commonly called brain death and is caused by interruption in the flow of blood or oxygen to the brain. At this point, the patient cannot think, feel anything, or breathe on his or her own.

THE BEGINNING OF TIME

The Greenwich meridian, or prime meridian, is also longitude zero and marks the starting point of every time zone in the world. Greenwich mean time is the mean—or average—time it takes the earth to rotate from noon to noon.

Since 1884, Greenwich mean time has also been known as world time, and sets official time around the globe. It is measured from the Greenwich meridian line (yes, there is an actual line on the ground) at the Royal Observatory at Greenwich, England. Hourly time signals from Greenwich Observatory were first broadcast on February 5, 1924.

Although Great Britain was the first nation to adopt a daylight saving plan, in 1908, Greenwich mean time forever remains the same all year round.

Countries and Territories Operating on Daylight Saving Time

NORTHERN HEMISPHERE

Albania	Cuba
Andorra	Cyprus
Armenia	Czech Republic
Austria	Denmark
Azerbaijan	Denmark—Faroe Islands
Bahamas	Denmark—Greenland
Belarus	Egypt
Belgium	Estonia
Bosnia and Herzegovina	Finland
Bulgaria	France
Canada	Gaza Strip
(except Saskatchewan)	Georgia
Croatia	Germany

Greece
Haiti
Hungary
Iran
Iraq
Ireland
Israel
Italy
Jordan
Kyrgyzstan
Latvia
Lebanon
Liechtenstein
Lithuania
Luxembourg
Macedonia
Malta
Mexico
Moldova
Monaco
Mongolia
Montenegro
Netherlands
Nicaragua
Norway
Poland
Portugal—Azores

Portugal—Madeira
Romania
Saint Pierre and Miquelon
San Marino
Serbia
Slovak Republic
Slovenia
Spain
Spain—Canary Islands
Sweden
Switzerland
Syria
Tunisia
Turkey
Turks and Caicos Islands
Ukraine
United Kingdom—Bermuda
United Kingdom—England
United Kingdom—Gibraltar
United Kingdom—Northern
    Ireland
United Kingdom—Scotland
United Kingdom—Wales
United States (except
    Hawaii, Arizona, part of
    Indiana)
Vatican City

SOUTHERN HEMISPHERE

Antarctica—Amundsen-Scott
    (South Pole)

Antarctica—McMurdo
    Station (United States)

Antarctica—Palmer Station (United States)	Chile
	Chile—Easter Island
Antarctica—Scott Station (New Zealand)	Namibia
	New Zealand
Australia—Lord Howe Island	New Zealand—Chatham Island
Australia—New South Wales	
Australia—South Australia	Paraguay
Australia—Tasmania	United Kingdom—Falkland Islands (Malvinas)
Australia—Victoria	
Brazil (part)	Uruguay

STICKY SOLUTION

It's a story of a dog and his burr. George de Mestral, tired of picking the prickly plant seed sacs from both his pooch and his pants after walking in the Alps, and curious as to their annoying sticking power, took off his trousers and put them under a microscope. Close examination showed that the small hooks on the burrs clung to the tiny loops of fabric. De Mestral found a way to manufacture this "locking tape" (he found that sewing nylon under infrared light formed indestructible hooks), and in 1948 decided to name it Velcro, a combination of the words "velvet" and "crochet."

The MELTING POINT of a solid is the same temperature as the freezing point of a liquid. This changes slightly with the addition of salt; it disrupts the molecular equilibrium, so that melting actually occurs faster than freezing.

MIGHTY WINDS
When It's This Windy, Watch Out!

Small craft advisory: A warning for sustained winds of 20–33 knots

Gale warning: A warning for sustained surface winds, or frequent gusts, in the range of 34–47 knots

Storm warning: A warning for sustained surface winds, or frequent gusts, in the range of 48–63 knots

Tropical storm warning: A warning for sustained surface winds, associated with a tropical cyclone, within the range of 34–63 knots

Hurricane-force wind warning: A warning for sustained winds, or frequent gusts, of 64 knots or greater

Hurricane warning: A warning for sustained surface winds of 64 knots or higher associated with a hurricane and expected in a specified coastal area within 24 hours or less; a hurricane or typhoon warning can remain in effect when dangerously high water or a combination of dangerously high water and exceptionally high waves continues, even though winds may be less than hurricane force.

◆

ON THE BLINK
Just When Do You Close Your Eyes for a Second and Miss Something?

A person generally blinks about nineteen times a minute. This is an average, and may differ if one is working in front of a computer, crying, or winking in a lascivious manner.

LEAVING IT ALL BEHIND?

In case you were thinking of leaving everything to your beloved
Fifi, you'd better figure out who's liable to outlive whom. Here
are estimated average life expectancies of some of our favorite
pets. (And in case you were wondering about human life expec-
tancy, it's presently near 75 years for men, and almost 80 for
women.)

DOGS

Airedale terrier	10 to 12 years
Beagle	12 to 15 years
Bloodhound	9 to 11 years
Border terrier	13 to 16 years
Boxer	9 to 11 years
Bull terrier	10 to 16 years
Cairn terrier	12 to 15 years
Chihuahua	15 to 18 years
Chow-chow	9 to 11 years
Cocker spaniel	14 to 16 years
Collie	12 to 15 years
Dachshund	15 to 18 years
Dalmatian	10 to 13 years
Doberman	12 to 15 years
German shepherd	10 to 13 years
Golden retriever	10 to 13 years
Great dane	7 to 10 years
Irish setter	14 to 16 years
Irish terrier	12 to 15 years
Newfoundland	7 to 10 years
Papillion	12 to 15 years
Pomeranian	12 to 15 years
Poodle	15 to 18 years

Schnauzer	14 to 16 years
Scottish terrier	12 to 15 years
St. Bernard	9 to 11 years
Wire fox terrier	12 to 14 years
Yorkshire terrier	12 to 15 years

CATS

Indoor	12 to 18 years
Outdoor	4 to 5 years

BIRDS

African gray parrot	50 to 60 years
Amazon	50 to 60 years
Budgie	10 to 15 years
Canary	7 to 9 years
Cockatiel	15 to 20 years
Cockatoo	up to 70 years
Lovebird	15 to 30 years
Macaw	up to 80 years
Parakeet	8 to 10 years

REPTILES AND AMPHIBIANS

Anole	4 years
Ball python	40 years
Bearded dragon	4 to 10 years
Boa constrictor	20 to 40 years
Chameleon	1 to 3 years
Corn snake	10 years
Frog	4 to 15 years
Iguana	15 years
King snake	20 years
Leopard Gecko	up to 20 years
Toad	20 years

Rodents

Chinchilla	15 years
Gerbil or hamster	3 years
Guinea pig	5 to 7 years
Mouse	3 to 4 years
Rabbit	5 to 15 years

Other

Pot-Bellied Pig	12 to 18 years
Sugar Glider	12 to 14 years
Tarantula	20 to 30 years

THE MAKINGS OF A SAINT

The process of becoming a Catholic saint is very lengthy, often taking decades—or even centuries—to complete. The steps to sainthood:

1. A local bishop investigates the candidate's life and writings for evidence of heroic virtue. The findings are sent on to the Vatican.
2. A panel of theologians and the cardinals of the Congregation for the Causes of Saints evaluate the candidate's life.
3. If the candidate is approved, the pope proclaims the person venerable, which means that he or she is a role model of Catholic virtues.
4. Beatification is the next step and is contingent on proof of a posthumous miracle by the candidate; the candidate is now also allowed to be honored by a particular group or region.
5. The final step for canonization is a second posthumous miracle. With this proof, the candidate in canonized in the Vatican as a saint.

"SIX BELLS AND ALL IS WELL!"

On board a ship, time is counted by the ringing of the ship's bell. The ship's crew takes turns being "on watch" in four-hour shifts* and rings the ship's bell every half hour (starting with one chime at 0030 hours military time, up to eight bells at 0400, then beginning with one bell again at 0430) to alert all keeping watch on different parts of the ship.

Watch	Twenty-four-Hour Clock	Twelve-Hour Clock
Middle	0000–0400	Midnight to 4 A.M.
Morning	0400–0800	4 A.M. to 8 A.M.
Forenoon	0800–1200	8 A.M. to noon
Afternoon	1200–1600	Noon to 4 P.M.
First Dog*	1600–1800	4 P.M. to 6 P.M.
Last Dog*	1800–2000	6 P.M. to 8 P.M.
First	2000–2400	8 P.M. to midnight

*Dog watches are only two hours long, to allow crew members to eat dinner.

Bell Time Sequence	Number of Rings
First half hour	One bell
First hour	Two bells
First hour and a half	Three bells
Second hour	Four bells
Second half-hour and a half	Five bells
Third hour	Six bells
Third hour and a half	Seven bells
Fourth hour	Eight bells

WHEN U.S. WORKS PASS INTO THE PUBLIC DOMAIN

Copyright

The U.S. Patent and Trademark Office defines a copyright as a form of protection provided to the authors of "original works of authorship," including literary, dramatic, musical, artistic, and certain other intellectual works, both published and unpublished.

Public Domain

A public domain work is a creative work that is not protected by copyright and which may be freely used by everyone. The reasons that the work is not protected include:

- The term of copyright for the work has expired.
- The author failed to satisfy statutory formalities to protect the copyright.
- The work is a work of the U.S. government.

Date of Work	Conditions	Term
Created January 1, 1978, or later	When work is fixed in tangible medium of expression	Life plus 70 years[1] (or if work of corporate authorship, the shorter of 95 years from publication, or 120 years from creation[2])
Published before 1923	In public domain	None

Published from 1923 to 1963	When published with notice	28 years plus could be renewed for 47 years, now extended by 20 years for a total renewal of 67 years. If not so renewed, is now in public domain
Published from 1964 to 1977	When published with notice[3]	28 years for first term; now automatic extension of 67 years for second term
Created before January 1, 1978, but not published	January 1, 1978, the effective date of the 1976 act, which eliminated common-law copyright	Life plus 70 years or December 31, 2002, whichever is greater
Created before January 1, 1978, but published between that date and December 31, 2002	January 1, 1978, the effective date of 1976 act, which eliminated common-law copyright	Life plus 70 years, or December 31, 2047, whichever is is greater

1. Term of joint works is measured by life of the longest-lived author.
2. Works for hire and anonymous and pseudonymous works also have this term (17 U.S.C. § 302[c]).
3. Under the 1909 act, works published without notice went into the public domain upon publication. Works published without notice between January 1, 1978, and March 1, 1989, the effective date of the Berne Convention Implementation Act, retained copyright only if efforts to correct the accidental omission of notice were made within five years, such as by placing notice on unsold copies (17 U.S.C. § 405).

"I DO," FOR NOW . . .
A Prenuptial Agreement Is Often Made When:

- You have assets such as a home, stock, or retirement funds
- You own all or part of a business
- You may receive an inheritance
- You have children or grandchildren, or both,
  from a previous marriage
- You are more financially stable than your betrothed
- You have family who need to be taken care of
- You are pursuing a degree in a potentially profitable
  profession, such as law or medicine
- You see a huge future for yourself

◆

KIDS TODAY!

Boys and girls truly *are* growing up earlier than ever before.
Females enter puberty between ages eight and thirteen,
though they may not menstruate for several years after this;
boys enter puberty between ages nine and fourteen. This
change is attributed to better health and nutrition; for
example, in North America the age of menstruation has
decreased by three to four months each decade after 1850.
Present U.S. statistics for growth increases are:

	Female Growth *Ages 10 to 14*	*Male Growth* *Ages 12 to 16*
Weight	15 to 55 pounds	15 to 65 pounds
Height	2 to 10 inches	4 to 12 inches
Age of puberty	8 to 13 years of age	9.5 to 14 years of age

WHEN are the call letters for SportsRadio 620 AM in Syracuse, New York.

◆

WHO SCREAMED FOR ICE CREAM?

Before there was ice cream (as unimaginable as that is), it seems that people were hard at work trying to invent it. History tells us that Alexander the Great (356–323 BCE) delighted in snow and ice covered with honey and nectar. Quite soon thereafter, in about 200 BCE, the Chinese were adding milk and a rice mixture to snow. Next came Emperor Nero Claudius Caesar (37–68 CE), who sent runners into the mountains to bring back snow, then flavored it with fruit and juices. And by the time of King Tang of Shang, China (618–697 CE), the recipe was improving: a little buffalo milk, flour, and camphor was added to the ice. By the mid-seventeenth century, Europeans were enjoying something they called creme ice, and the first ice cream parlor in the United States appeared in New York City in 1776.

◆

Just over one hundred years ago, the population of LAS VEGAS, NEVADA, was thirty people.

◆

SKY LIGHT

Edmond Halley (1656–1742) predicted that the comet the world saw in 1531, 1607, and 1682 would return in 1758. He was right, and the comet was named for him posthumously. His calculations proved that the comet's average orbit is seventy-six years; its last sighting was in 1986, so we can expect the next sky show in 2061.

SHINE ON

Every September, skywatchers observe a special phenomenon in the sky: the harvest moon. It's no ordinary full moon: throughout the year the moon rises on a completely different schedule than the sun, on average about 50 minutes later each night. But near the autumnal equinox, the retardation of the moon's rising has sunset and moonrise nearly coinciding for a few special evenings. Because it comes in handy for farmers working long days to harvest their crops before a frost, the extra dose of lighting afforded by the full moon gave the harvest moon its name. If the sky is unclouded, there is full moonlight from sunset to sunrise.

The Farmers Almanac gave every month's full moon a very colorful, yet descriptive name:

January	Wolf Moon
February	Snow Moon
March	Worm Moon
April	Pink Moon
May	Flower Moon
June	Strawberry Moon
July	Buck Moon
August	Sturgeon Moon
September	Harvest Moon
October	Hunter's Moon
November	Beaver Moon
December	Cold Moon

◆

In the course of one year, the average person has more than 1,460 DREAMS.

AFTER SINGING AULD LANG SYNE
...How to say "Happy New Year!" in far-flung places:

Language	Happy New Year!
Afrikaans	Voorspoedige nuwe jaar
Arabic	Kul 'am wa antum bikhair
Basque	Urte Berri on
Bengali	Shuvo noboborsho
Chinese (Mandarin)	Xin nian yu kuai
Czech	Stastny Novy Rok
Dutch	Gelukkig nieuwjaar
Esperanto	Bonan Novjaron
Finnish	Onnellista uutta vuotta
Greek	Eutychismenos o kainourgios chronos
Hawaiian	Hauoli Makahiki hou
Hebrew	Shana Tova
Hungarian	Boldog uj evet
Indonesian (Bahasa)	Selamat Tahun Baru
Italian	Felice Anno Nuovo or Buon anno
Japanese	Akemashite Omedetou Gozaimasu
Korean	Sehe Bokmanee Bateuseyo
Laotian (Hmong)	Nyob Zoo Xyoo Tshiab
Latin	Felix sit annus novus
Nigerian (Hausa)	Barka da sabuwar shekara
Norwegian	Godt Nytt År
Philippines (Tagalog)	Manigong Bagong Taon
Polish	Szczesliwego Nowego Roku
Romanian	La Multi Ani si Un An Nou Fericit
Samoan	Ia manuia le Tausaga Fou
Swahili	Heri za Mwaka Mpya
Swedish	Gott Nytt År
Vietnamese	Chuc mung nam moi
Welsh	Blwyddyn Newydd Dda

PUTTING ON THE FEEDBAG
A Food Timeline: The Discovery of Culinary Delights
We Couldn't Live Without

Date	*Food*	*Where Discovered*
6000 BCE	Wine	Iran
6000 BCE	Cheese	Iraq
4000 BCE	Watermelon	Egypt
3600 BCE	Popcorn	Mexico
2000 BCE	Marshmallows*	Egypt
1500 BCE	Chocolate	Mexico
490 BCE	Pasta	Italy
1300 CE	Guacamole	Mexico
1475 CE	Pork and Beans	Italy
1475 CE	Coffee	Turkey
1592 CE	Pot luck	England
1650 CE	Rum	Caribbean Islands
1754 CE	Swedish meatballs	Sweden
1784 CE	Lollipops	England
1826 CE	Fondue	Switzerland
1927 CE	Pez	Austria
1953 CE	Peeps*	United States

*It took nearly four thousand years for the civilized world to progress from plain marshmallows to Peeps, though to be fair, the Peep is not actually made from marshmallow. Until the mid-nineteenth century, marshmallow candies were indeed made with the sap of the root of the marsh-mallow plant (*althea officinalis*). Since then, gelatin has taken its place.

◆

MAMIE SMITH recorded the first vocal blues song, "Crazy Blues," in 1920.

PLAY BALL!

Talk about opening day! April 20, 1912, was the first day at
two of America's longest-lasting ballparks: Fenway Park in
Boston, home of the Red Sox, and now-defunct Detroit's
Tiger Stadium.

SCRAPING THE SKY

Though only ten stories tall, Chicago's Home Insurance
Building, built in 1885 and designed by William LeBaron
Jenney (1832–1907), is considered the first true skyscraper.
While the marriage of a steel framework combined with
masonry gave way to tall buildings like the Home Insurance
Building, the load-bearing capacity problem that stood in the
way of truly enormous height was only solved when a system
was invented in which the metal framework supported both
the floors and the walls. Because of his work in this field, it is
George A. Fuller (1851–1900), and not Jenney, who is credited
as the "inventor" of the skyscraper; in fact, the Flatiron
Building in New York City was formerly named the Fuller
Building.

HANDS ON

Watches and clocks are often displayed with the hands at
either 10:10 or 7:22. Theorists say the former is found mostly
in the display of clocks and watches because the symmetry is
pleasing to the eye. As to the latter time, which is often seen
on displayed antique timepieces, legend has it that it's a
tribute to Abraham Lincoln. The time of his death was 7:22
A.M., April 15, 1865.

"GIVE ME YOUR POOR . . ."

An inconsequential dot of land in New York Harbor known as
Gull Island was first purchased by the colonist governors of
Nieuw Amsterdam (later New York) from Native Americans
on July 12, 1630, for "certain cargoes, or parcels of goods."
And from 1894 to 1954 it took in over 16 million pieces of
precious cargo indeed: the immigrants who came through
what is now known as Ellis Island. Today, more than 100
million people count themselves descendants of someone who
came through Ellis Island's Registry Room.

1620s	Dutch settlers name the island Oyster Island after finding beds nearby.
1785	The current owner, Samuel Ellis, tries unsuccessfully to sell the property; it is sold to New York after his death in 1807.
1808	The U.S. government buys Ellis Island from New York for $10,000.
1813	Ellis Island becomes known as Fort Gibson and houses huge amounts of ammunition.
1847	The first proposal to make Fort Gibson a stopping place for incoming immigrants is made; the U.S. government opts for Castle Garden instead.
1861	Fort Gibson is dismantled; the land is renamed Ellis Island.
1890	The federal government establishes the Bureau of Immigration; Ellis Island is chosen as the site for a new federal immigration station for the port of New York.

1892	The immigration station on Ellis Island is opened on January 1.
1907	11,747 immigrants pass through Ellis Island in one day—1,025,000 will be the record-breaking number of immigrants who pass through the doors in this year.
1924	The number of immigrants passing through Ellis Island begins to decrease.
1943	Ellis Island is used as a detention center for enemy aliens.
1954	Ellis Island officially closes and is offered for bid.
1965	Ellis Island is classified as a National Monument in conjunction with the Statue of Liberty National Monument.
1990	The Ellis Island Immigration Museum opens on September 10.

◆

THE BIRDS

Though legend has it that the swallows return to San Juan Capistrano every year on March 19, scientists insist that what some perceive as a miracle is less mysterious than meets the eye. The birds do return to build their nests in the old mission every year some time near the vernal equinox, and depart around October 23 for their six-thousand-mile journey south to Goya, Corrientes, Argentina. But, as with aviary migration in general, scientists know little more than the fact that weather and the lack of food are the main factors governing when birds take flight.

GIVE ME YOUR CASH

A Chemical Bank in Rockville Centre, New York, was the first bank to feature an automated teller machine in 1969. It was not exactly a "teller": it dispensed only cash. Today, the average American visits an ATM on an average of five times per month.

◆

How often does LIGHTNING strike? About six thousand times per minute worldwide.

◆

HOORAY FOR HOLLYWOODLAND

In 1923, the Hollywoodland Real Estate Group erected a temporary sign up in the terrain of the Hollywood Hills to advertise a housing development of the same name. It cost $21,000 and was meant to last less than two years. Each letter of the "HOLLYWOODLAND" sign initially stood four stories high, at fifty feet, and was thirty feet along the base; the sign was lit by four thousand lightbulbs, and a nearby cabin housed a maintenance man whose sole job was to change them.

The years went by, and the company has long since gone under, but the locals loved the sign and the movie industry—the whole idea of "Hollywood"—had captured America's imagination. There's still no easy way to reach the sign. It's not on a road, it's fenced in to keep out the curious, and it's fitted with a new high-tech alarm system. It's maintained by the Hollywood Sign Trust, whose trustees are named by the Hollywood Chamber of Commerce and the City of Los Angeles. Today it reads just "HOLLYWOOD," but it means a whole lot more.

WHEN IT'S GOOD, IT'S VERY, VERY GOOD . . .

But when it's bad, it's horrid! Here are guidelines used by many manufacturers for food consumption.

- Dating is not federally required, except for infant formula and baby food.
- States have varying laws. Most states require that milk and other perishables be sold before the expiration date.
- Stores are not legally required to remove other food from their shelves once the expiration date has passed. The dates are only advisory in nature.

A Guide to the System

Sell By:	Don't buy the product after this date. This is what we think of as the expiration date.
Best If Used By:	Flavor or quality is best by this date, but the product is still edible thereafter.
Use By:	The last day that the manufacturer vouches for the product's quality.

◆

NOTHING TO CELEBRATE
U.S. Holidays with the Most Alcohol-Related Traffic Fatalities

1. New Year's Eve
2. New Year's Day
3. Super Bowl Sunday
4. St. Patrick's Day
5. Memorial Day
6. Fourth of July
7. Labor Day Weekend
8. Halloween
9. Thanksgiving
10. Christmas

BUBONIC PLAGUE

The history of the plague is terrifying and its sword was swift. It was said that people "ate lunch with their friends and dinner with their ancestors in paradise."

1330s: Bubonic plague begins in the Gobi Desert of China, killing 35 million Asians. Fleas that make their homes on infected rats are the culprits.

1347: Italian merchants return from trips to the Black Sea, infected with the plague.

1352: By now, 25 percent of Europe's population is wiped out—approximately 25 million people.

1400–1542: The plague makes sporadic appearances in Italy, France, and Turkey.

1665: The plague reappears in London; within a year, 15 percent of the city's population is dead.

1892: The plague spreads from China to India, killing more than 6 million people in India alone.

1900–1909: A small outbreak of plague hits San Francisco. It is finally wiped out with the help of the 1906 earthquake and a 1907 bounty on rats.

1980s: The United States averages eighteen cases of plague per year; with the advent of antibiotics, fatalities are only one in seven.

Today, between one thousand and two thousand cases of plague are reported worldwide, mostly in rural areas, and due to infected rats.

THE FLAG AT HALF-MAST

The United States flag may be flown at half-mast to represent the death of a government official, unless otherwise specified by the president. It should first be hoisted to the peak for an instant and then lowered to the half-staff position; it should be raised to the peak again before it is lowered for the day. The flag is never to be displayed with the union down, except as a signal of dire distress in instances of extreme danger to life or property, for instance, if a crew abandons ship. Half-staff etiquette from the federal law known as the Flag Code calls for:

- Thirty days for a president (current or former)

- Ten days for the vice president, chief justice of the Supreme Court (current or former), Speaker of the House

- From day of death until interment for an associate justice of the Supreme Court, secretary of an executive or military department, former vice president, governor of a state, territory, or possession

- On the day of death and the following day for a member of Congress

- On Memorial Day (last Monday of May in the United States), the flag is traditionally displayed at half-mast from dawn until noon and at full mast for the remainder of daylight hours

- Additionally, the flag should be lighted at all times, either by sunlight between dawn and dusk, or by an appropriate light source after dark.

WHEN "WHEN" MAKES THE DIFFERENCE
A Few Words on "When"

Of all cold words of tongue or pen
The worst are these: "I knew him when—"
—ARTHUR GUITERMAN (1871–1943)

When men drink, then they are rich and successful and win
lawsuits and are happy and help their friends.
Quickly, bring me a beaker of wine, so that I may wet my
mind and say something clever.
—ARISTOPHANES (CA. 450–385 BCE)

We are of course a nation of differences.
These differences don't make us weak. They're the source of
our strength. . . . The question is not when we came here . . .
but why our families came here. And what we did after we
arrived.
—JAMES EARL (JIMMY) CARTER JR. (1924–)

I have been here before,
But when or how I cannot tell;
I know the grass beyond the door,
The sweet keen smell,
The sighing sound, the lights around the shore.
—DANTE GABRIEL ROSSETTI (1828–1882)

First Witch: "When shall we three meet again
In thunder, lightning, or in rain?"
Second Witch: "When the hurlyburly's done,
When the battle's lost and won."
—WILLIAM SHAKESPEARE (1564–1616), MACBETH

What never has been, yet may have its when;
The thing which has been, never is again.
—JAMES THOMSON (1834–1882)

Where have all the flowers gone?
The girls have picked them, every one.
Oh, when will they ever learn?
—PETER (PETE) SEEGER (1919–)

◆

HEAVY-TECH

Adam Osbourne, an ex-publisher turned computer geek, started the short-lived Osbourne Computers and in 1981 produced the Osbourne 1, considered by many to be the first laptop computer. It had a five-inch screen, a modem port, and two floppy drives, weighed in at twenty-four pounds, and cost $1,795.

ALIEN INVASION

Nuremberg, Germany, 1561: The *Nuremberg Gazette* reported a variety of UFOs—a "frightful spectacle," noted observers. Though not, perhaps, what we today think of as an alien invasion, there were reports of a sky filled with "cylindrical shapes from which emerged black, red, orange and blue-white spheres that darted about," and a "black, spear-like object" appeared.

◆

One hundred years ago, 95 percent of all BIRTHS in the United States took place at home.

ONE LEG AT A TIME

In 1872, tailor Jacob Davis contacted dry-goods entrepreneur Levi Strauss about producing a sturdy pair of pants, using metal rivets to hold them together. The two men received a patent for an "Improvement in Fastening Pocket-Openings," put their heads together, and the "waist overall," or modern-day jeans as we know them, was born.

◆

Just over one hundred years ago, in 1904, the five leading CAUSES OF DEATH in the United States were:

1. Pneumonia and influenza
2. Tuberculosis
3. Diarrhea
4. Heart disease
5. Stroke

◆

NUMBER, PLEASE, MR. OSCAR?

Since 1949, starting with the somewhat arbitrary number 501, each Oscar statuette has borne a serial number behind its heels.

DAY IS DONE

The bugle call "Taps" was written by Brigadier General Daniel Butterfield in 1862, and though it is played during funerals and flag ceremonies as well, it is used in the military at the end of every day to signal "lights out," replacing Tatoo, the French bugle call. "Taps" was immediately adopted by both Union and Confederate forces.

In 1851 the first issue of *The New York Times* was published as the NEW YORK DAILY TIMES.

◆

THE FABRIC OF OUR LIVES

In the fourteenth century, hand painting on cotton cloth, both freehand and stencil, became popular in India. Europeans began importing this fabric, mostly an early chintz, because it laundered easily, was lightweight, and featured bright, cheerful colors. Soon both the design and the variety of new fabrics coming out of India reflected European tastes. Countries such as England and France made it illegal to import these Indian goods and began manufacturing their own textiles, cornering the market for both clothing and furniture. By the 1790s, England, France, Germany, Switzerland, and the Netherlands all had busy textile mills of their own.

GOOD EV-EN-INGS

For half a century, Alfred Hitchcock peppered his films with brief and comical cameo appearances: thirty-seven films in all, forty cameos. Hats and musical instruments were often part of his guise, but whether with a familiar prop or skulking in the background, catching a glimpse of the famous director is one of the most enjoyable aspects of many Hitchcock films. Only once did he have a cameo on his TV show, *Alfred Hitchcock Presents*, aside from his onstage introductions. In an episode titled "Dip in the Pool," he is pictured on the cover of a magazine. Following, a list of the forty Hitchcock cameos (some have two) in these thirty-seven films:

Film	Year	Prop
The Lodger	1927	(1) none
		(2) gray cap
Easy Virtue	1927	cane
Blackmail	1929	reading book with a small boy
Murder!	1930	with a female companion
The 39 Steps	1935	tossing litter
Young and Innocent	1937	camera
The Lady Vanishes	1938	cigarette
Foreign Correspondent	1940	hotel
Rebecca	1940	none
Mr. & Mrs. Smith	1941	none
Suspicion	1941	none
Saboteur	1942	none
Shadow of a Doubt	1943	playing cards
Lifeboat	1944	none
Spellbound	1945	violin
Notorious	1946	champagne
The Paradine Case	1947	cello
Rope	1948	(1) none
		(2) none
Under Capricorn	1949	(1) none
		(2) none

Cameo	Minutes into Film
newsroom desk	3
in crowd at arrest	92
walking past tennis court	15
subway car	11
outside murder scene	60
outside theater	7
photographer at courthouse	15
Victoria Station platform	90
outside Johnny Jones' newspaper	11
walking past phone booth	123
outside Smiths' apartment building	41
at village mailbox	45
at newsstand, behind saboteur's car	60
on train to Santa Rosa	17
in newspaper ad in bottom of lifeboat	25
Empire State Building elevator	36
Alex Sebastian's party	64
Cumberland Station train	36
man crossing street	during opening credits
neon silhouette	52
at Sydney parade	3
steps of government house	14

Film	Year	Prop
Stage Fright	1950	none
Strangers on a Train	1951	bass fiddle
I Confess	1953	none
Rear Window	1954	none
Dial M for Murder	1954	none
To Catch a Thief	1955	none
The Trouble with Harry	1955	none
The Man Who Knew Too Much	1956	none
The Wrong Man	1956	none
Vertigo	1958	horn case
North by Northwest	1959	none
Psycho	1960	cowboy hat
The Birds	1963	white terriers
Marnie	1964	none
Torn Curtain	1966	baby on lap
Topaz	1969	in wheelchair
Frenzy	1972	bowler hat
Family Plot	1976	none

Cameo	Minutes into Film
staring at Eve Gill in maid's disguise on street	38
boarding a train	10
top of steps in Quebec	1
repairing clock in musician's apartment	25
class-reunion picture taken off wall	13
sitting near John Robie on bus	10
walking past outdoor art exhibition	21
Morroccan marketplace just before murder	25
onscreen prologue (only onscreen cameo as himself)	film opening
walking across shipyard	10
just missing bus	2
outside Marion Crane's realty office	7
leaving pet shop	2
coming out of hotel room	5
sitting in hotel lobby	8
LaGuardia Airport	28
in crowd at political rally	3
in silhouette outside office	40

WORLD'S OLDEST

When things in our world are *so* old, they're *olde*. A few firsts throughout time . . .

World's Oldest City
Damascus, in Syria, is the world's oldest continuously inhabited city, having been lived in since pre-second millennium BCE.

World's Oldest Backgammon Set
The oldest backgammon board in the world, along with sixty pieces, was unearthed beneath the rubble of the five-thousand-year-old Burnt City in Iran. The intricate board features an engraved serpent coiling around itself twenty times, thus producing twenty slots for game play.

World's Oldest Church
The ruins of the world's most ancient Christian church are from about 350 in Jordan, a few hundred yards from the Red Sea in the Christian community of Ayla, a Roman city damaged by an earthquake.

Oldest City in the United States
Since 1513 St. Augustine, Florida, has been the oldest continuously settled city in the United States. The Spanish explorer Juan Ponce de León, in search of the legendary Fountain of Youth, landed there and took possession of the territory for Spain.

World's Oldest Rodeo
Since July 4, 1888, in Prescott, Arizona, "cowboy tournaments" have had folks saddling up, though the word "rodeo" wasn't actually used until 1916.

World's Oldest Mouse
Yoda, the world's oldest mouse, lived an amazing four years and twelve days, or roughly 136 human years. A dwarf mouse, Yoda's obit reported that he lived in quiet seclusion with his cage mate, Princess Leia.

World's Oldest Volcanic Rock
Rocks found by geologists in Porpoise Cove on the shores of Canada's Hudson Bay are estimated to be 3.825 billion years old (plus or minus 16 million years). The earth is thought to be 4.6 billion years old.

World's Oldest Lake
Lake Baikal, or "Sacred Sea," located in southeastern Siberia, is 25–30 million years old, and holds more than 20 percent of the world's fresh water.

World's Oldest Wine Jar
The world's earliest known ancient wine jar dates from ca. 5400–5000 BCE and was discovered in 1968 in the "kitchen" of a mud-brick Neolithic building in Hajji Firuz Tepe, Iran.

World's Oldest Insect
The fossilized jaw remains found of the oldest known living insect belong to the winged Rhyniognatha hirsti, which lived between 408 and 436 million years ago. A professor rediscovered it in a London museum drawer in 2004, where it had been lying, unidentified, since 1928.

World's Oldest Pet Cat
The remains of a human and a cat were found buried together in 2004 in a 9,500-year-old grave on Cyprus, leading scientists to believe they found the world's oldest known pet cat.

World's Oldest Ice

The oldest ice ever found was taken from a deep hole in
Antarctica in 2005; it will help scientists determine the history
of the world's climate. The ice dates back 900,000 years, to
when modern mammals ruled the earth, but hominids had not
yet evolved beyond the *Homo erectus* stage.

World's Oldest Tree

Methuselah, a 4,768-year-old bristlecone pine discovered in
1957, lives in a secret location in the Schulman Grove in
California's Inyo National Forest.

World's Oldest Gorilla

Rudy, a lowland gorilla born in 1956 and captured as a baby in
Africa, resided in the Erie, Pennsylvania, zoo until March 9,
2005, when he passed away at the age of forty-nine.

World's Oldest Pile of Vomit

Paleontologists discovered mounds of fossilized Jurassic
throw-up from ichthyosaurs that swam in the waters of
England 160 million years ago. It is believed that these marine
reptiles ate shellfish—just as sperm whales do—and then
vomited the indigestible shells. The evidence of the
dinosaurs' postprandial discomfort is extremely important for
scientists' research on their eating habits.

World's Oldest Grapevine

Maribor, Slovenia's second-largest city, is home to an annual
grape harvest taken from a four-hundred-year-old grapevine.
The grapes are still ripened into wine, bottled in small bottles,
and used as special official presents.

World's Oldest Kitchen

In 2003, stone tools between 2.5 million and 2.6 million years old were discovered in Gona, Ethiopia, in the Awash Valley. The remains from simple knives, and the proximity to a river, plus animals bones found nearby, have scientists believing this to be the site of the oldest known kitchen.

World's Oldest Camp
In 1885, the YMCA opened Camp Dudley, in Westport, New York, making it the oldest continuously running YMCA summer camp for boys.

World's Oldest Wheel
A wooden wheel uncovered in marshes outside of Ljubljana, Slovenia, is between 5,100 and 5,350 years old.

World's Oldest Rice
Archaeologists discovered in Korea a handful of burnt grains of domesticated rice more than 15,000 years old. This find challenges the once-accepted fact that rice cultivation originated in China 12,000 years ago.

World's Oldest Flower
Researchers believe they have discovered fossil evidence of a 142-million-year-old flower. This spindly twig with peapod-shaped fruit and a woody stem was found in the limestone and volcanic ash layers of a rock formation in China.

◆

PUZZLING . . .

European mapmakers were the originators of jigsaw puzzles in the 1760s, pasting maps onto wood and cutting them into small pieces.

THEY'RE HERE . . .

On June 24, 1947, pilot Kenneth Arnold noticed nine disk-shaped objects not far from Mount Rainier in Washington State when he was searching for a lost plane. This is the first reported UFO sighting in the United States, and a journalist's mistake in citing Arnold's description of the event brought about the term "flying saucers." "I said that they flew like they take a saucer and throw it across the water," Arnold later reported to veteran newsman Edward R. Murrow. "Most of the newspapers misunderstood and misquoted that. . . . They said that I said that they were saucer-like; I said that they flew in a saucer-like fashion." No wonder confusion still reigns in the realm of extraterrestrials.

HOW LONG HAS THIS BEEN GOING ON?

An eon is a division of time so long it's, well, timeless. Various definitions include:

the longest unit of geological time, next in order of magnitude above an era
an immeasurably long period of time
a very long period of time
two or more eras

◆

HINDUISM is the world's oldest continuously practiced religion.

DISCO MADNESS

Though many tunes and their new sound paved the way for disco—"The Theme from Shaft" and Love Unlimited's "Love Theme," both from 1971, are often cited—most musical experts agree that 1972's "Soul Makossa" by Manu Dibango is the first real disco song.

By 1974, mixmaster Tom Moulton made two huge contributions to disco. For Gloria Gaynor's first album, "Never Can Say Goodbye," Moulton mixed a medley of three songs into a dance mix that lasted the whole length of one album side. The next year, Moulton and recording engineer José Rodriguez took that one step further, by making the first twelve-inch single as a promotional item for nightclub DJs. By 1976, twelve-inch singles were released for public consumption, and a new kind of disco inferno took over. Yet by the end of the decade, mirror balls were coming down, as the disco era was on its way out.

◆

An EARTHQUAKE on December 16, 1811, in the Mississippi Valley near New Madrid, Missouri, caused parts of the Mississippi River to actually flow backward. It was so severe that it's said the quake made church bells ring in Boston; on the Mississippi, boats were found forty miles upstream of where they had been moored, as the river rushed to fill a depression nearly one hundred miles long from the earthquake. In fact, Arkansas's St. Francis Lake was formed by the New Madrid earthquake.

Recent activity along the New Madrid fault has been much less dramatic. A quake on September 17, 1997, was measured at a magnitude of 3.8 on the Richter scale.

A TIME OF HORROR

"Arbeit Macht Frei" ("Work Makes You Free") was the appalling motto of the Nazi concentration camps that were spread throughout Europe; astonishingly, many existed from the 1930s until their liberation at the end of World War II.

Auschwitz-Birkenau (1940–1945)
Poland
Annihilation camp; forced-labor camp
2.1 million–2.5 million killed
Liberated by the Soviet Union
Camp preserved

Belzec (1942–1943)
Poland
Annihilation camp
500,000–600,000 killed
Liquidated by Germany
Monument

Bergen-Belsen (1943–1945)
Germany
Holding center
50,000 killed
Liberated by the United Kingdom
Graveyard

Buchenwald (1937–1945)
Germany
Forced-labor camp
56,000 killed
Liberated by the United States
Camp preserved; museum

CHELMNO (1943–1945)
Poland
Annihilation camp
150,000–300,000 killed
Liquidated by Germany
Monument

DACHAU (1933–1945)
Germany
Forced-labor camp
32,000 killed
Liberated by the United States
Camp preserved; museum

DORA/MITTELBAU (1943–1945)
Germany
Forced-labor camp
20,000 killed
Liberated by the United States
Memorial Sculpture Plaza

FLOSSENBÜRG (1938–1945)
Germany
Forced-labor camp
73,000 killed
Liberated by the United States
Buildings; monument

GROSS-ROSEN (1940–1945)
Poland
Forced-labor camp
40,000 killed
Liberated by the Soviet Union
Camp preserved; museum

JANOWSKA (1941–1943)
Ukraine
Forced-labor camp; annihilation camp
40,000 killed
Liquidated by Germany
Not maintained

KAISERWALD (1943–1944)
Latvia
Forced-labor camp
10,000 killed
Liquidated by Germany
Not maintained

MAJDANEK (1941–1944)
Poland
Annihilation camp
360,000 killed
Liberated by the Soviet Union
Camp preserved; monument

MAUTHAUSEN (1938–1945)
Austria
Forced-labor camp
150,000 killed
Liberated by the United States
Buildings; monument

NATZWEILER/STRUTHOF (1941–1944)
France
Forced-labor camp
10,000 killed
Liquidated by Germany
Camp preserved

NEUENGAMME (1940–1945)
Germany
Forced-labor camp
56,000 killed
Liberated by the United Kingdom
Used as prison; monument

ORANIENBURG (1930–1935)
Germany
Holding center
105,000 killed
Liquidated by Germany
Not maintained

PLASZOW (1942–1945)
Poland
Forced-labor camp
8,000 killed
Liquidated by Germany
Not maintained

RAVENSBRÜCK (1939–1945)
Germany
Forced-labor camp
92,000 killed
Liberated by the Soviet Union
Buildings; monument

SACHSENHAUSEN (1936–1945)
Germany
Forced-labor camp
30,000–35,000 killed
Liberated by the Soviet Union
Museum; buildings

SOBIBOR (1942–1943)
Poland
Annihilation camp
250,000 killed
Liquidated by Germany
Monument

STUTTHOF (1939–1945)
Poland
Forced-labor camp
85,000 killed
Liberated by the Soviet Union
Buildings; museum

TEREZIN (THERESIENSTADT) (1941–1945)
Czech Republic
Holding center transit ghetto
35,000 killed
Liberated by the Soviet Union
Buildings; monument

TREBLINKA (1942–1943)
Poland
Annihilation camp
265,000 killed
Liquidated by Germany
Monument

WESTERBORK (1939–1945)
Netherlands
Transit camp
Unknown number of deaths
Liberated by Canada
Monument

OLYMPIAN FEATS

In 1936, Jesse Owens ruined Adolf Hitler's grand design to make the Berlin Olympics an Aryan showcase when the African American brought home four gold medals in the 100- and 200-meter dashes, the long jump, and the 4-by-100 relay team. But he was not the first black man to capture an Olympic medal for the United States: In 1904, George Coleman Poage won two bronzes in the St. Louis Olympics for the 220- and 440-yard hurdles.

"THE DEVIL'S ROPE"

By 400 CE, smooth wire was being made, but not until the nineteenth century was it manufactured and available in enough quantity for wide use. On its heels came the invention of barbed wire—and the agricultural future of the United States changed completely. By 1873, Joseph F. Glidden (1813–1906) had applied for a patent for barbed wire, the simple barrier that was perhaps the single most important invention in ranching history. The only drawback? It took some time for livestock to get used to the new fences, and the results were bloody. Protesting religious groups began to call it "The Devil's Rope."

SING!

In 1927, *Show Boat* made its debut as the first Broadway musical play. It was an adaptation of the popular Edna Ferber novel.

INAUGURAL LUNCHEON

It should be the meal of a lifetime for a new president. But apparently, even the leader of the free world can't always get what he wants . . .

Franklin Delano Roosevelt knew exactly what he wanted for his 1945 inauguration luncheon, and on the face of it, the request seemed quite modest: The commander in chief desired chicken à la king. First Lady Eleanor intervened, however, with unfortunate results. Between her lack of culinary taste, and a parsimonious housekeeper, the menu for the two thousand guests looked like this:

Chicken Salad
Rolls, unbuttered
Pound Cake, unfrosted
Coffee

Cut to 2001 and the inaugural luncheon for President George W. Bush—and a Texas-sized menu:

Lobster Pie—Morsels of lobster sautéed with fresh herbs and winter vegetables in a rich cream sauce; served in a flaky pastry crust, topped with fresh lobster, garnished with lemon leaves and lemon wedges

Grenadine of Beef Supreme—Petit filets of prime beef tenderloin individually tied, marinated in garlic and fresh herbs, interlayered with well-seasoned and sautéed vegetables, topped with a turned mushroom cap, and presented over steamed green beans with Madeira demiglace

Chartreuse of Vegetables—A puff pastry ring filled with chestnuts, Brussels sprouts, and parisienne vegetables

including carrots, squash, broccoli stems, zucchini, and
yellow and red tomatoes

Puree of Small Roots—Celery root, turnips, and parsnips

Sour Cream Drop Biscuits—Served warm

Toffee Pudding—A moist, dense nutmeat pudding loaf served
with caramel sauce, surrounded with navel and blood orange
slices topped with crystallized ginger and sugared pecans and
presented warm with very rich vanilla bean ice cream scoops

Demitasse Cafe and Tea

Chocolate-dipped ginger, candied fruit rinds, fresh
strawberries, macaroons, and truffles

THAR SHE BLOWS!

On January 3, 1841, Herman Melville embarked on a whaling
voyage from Fairhaven, Massachusetts, aboard the whaling
ship *Acushnet*. He jumped ship after eighteen months, finding
that the sea was less to his liking than it was to his fictional
monomaniac, Captain Ahab. The experience served him well
a decade later, however, when he sat down to write his
masterpiece, *Moby-Dick*. Incredibly, that literary voyage took
him but a year.

UNDER THE KNIFE

In 1787, Austria became the first country to abolish capital
punishment. However, it was reinstituted for a time during
the reign of Hitler; between 1938 and 1945, 1,377 men and
women were guillotined for opposing the Nazis and for
treason.

A BRIEF PUBLISHING TIMELINE

The alphabet, the invention of paper, the printing press, the first potboiler: the written word is unique to the human race—it is what defines us. Herewith just a few of the many moments when the written word has changed the world.

1700 BCE: Phoenicians develop the first surviving alphabet, which consisted of twenty-two consonants and no vowels.

1270 BCE: The first general encyclopedia is written in Syria.

530 BCE: Pisistratus, son of Hippocrates, establishes the first public library in Athens.

131 BCE: *Acta Diurna (Daily Events)*, a daily gazette comparable to the modern newspaper. First created for general reading, then published regularly under Julius Caesar in 59 BCE.

100–200 CE: Lucius Apuleius writes "Cupid and Psyche" and includes it in *The Golden Ass*; scholars consider this to be the first literary fairy tale, similar to *Beauty and the Beast*.

105 CE: Ts'ai Lun, an official of the Chinese imperial court, invents paper—and forever changes the way we learn.

868: The earliest dated printed book is a Chinese translation of the Diamond Sutra and is printed with plates made from carved wood blocks.

1007: A Japanese noblewoman, Murasaki Shikibu, writes the world's first full novel, *The Tale of Genji*.

1450: Johannes Gutenberg invents the first mechanical printing press, an idea he derived from the olive press.

1452: Gutenberg conceives the idea for a press with movable type, which is individual letters cast on independent metal bodies; this affords easy assembly into blocks for printing, and the type can be constantly rearranged for further usage.

1611: In England, the King's Printer, Christopher Barker, prints the Authorized Version of the King James Bible, a uniform translation in the vernacular for the people, written by the greatest scholars of the day.

1675: John Foster, America's first engraver, sets up the first U.S. press in Boston, Massachusetts.

1709: The Statute of Anne is the first copyright act in the world and introduced the concept of an author being the owner of copyright, and the principle of a fixed term of protection for published works.

1714: Englishman Henry Mill receives the first patent for a typewriter, though his invention won't become popularized for more than a century.

1731: The first American circulating library opens in Philadelphia.

1754: Benjamin Franklin creates the first cartoon published in an American newspaper: a severed snake, representing the states, with the legend "Join, or Die."

1824: Louis Braille creates a method of writing and printing for the blind.

1886: The linotype typesetting machine is patented by Ottmar Mergenthaler; characters can now be cast in metal type as a complete line, rather than as individual characters.

1886: The Berne Convention devises an agreement of mutual recognition among nations, which maintains that a book that is copyrighted in any signatory state is also copyrighted in all the other signatory states under exactly the same conditions as a book first published in that country.

1896: The first comic book, Richard Fenton Outcalt's *The Yellow Kid*, appears in America.

1922: James Joyce's *Ulysses* is published in Paris and is immediately banned in both the United States and England until the 1930s. Though the first edition contained more than two thousand errors, it remains the most accurate edition ever published.

1966: Jacqueline Susann's *Valley of the Dolls* is published, and the steamy blockbuster is born.

2000: Author Stephen King publishes *Riding the Bullet*, the first electronic book to appear exclusively on the Internet. Though it never appeared in printed book form, it was released as a movie in 2004.

FOOD ON THE MOVE

The Pig Stand was the first drive-in restaurant and came on the scene before most Americans even owned cars; it eventually became a local fast-food chain located in Dallas, Texas. Back in 1921, it was a hopping spot—car-hopping, that is. Curb service was available in the parking lot, food production was speedy, and the Pig Stand even had a theme: barbecue, of course.

A fetus develops FINGERPRINTS at twenty-four weeks.

THE LAST NAIL

A great event in transportation occurred at Promontory, Utah, on May 10, 1869, as the Union Pacific tracks joined those of the Central Pacific Railroad, and "The Golden Spike"—the last spike, which would connect the two railroads—was driven. The excitement was so dizzying and the crowd so huge that hardly anyone could see the spike actually being hammered; but a single word went out from the site via Morse code to the rest of the world: "Done."

Then, in 1942, an event few remember: The old rails over the 123-mile Promontory Summit Line were derailed and salvaged for the war effort, and a ceremony marking the "Undriving of the Golden Spike" took place. Since then, Congress has established a Golden Spike National Historic Park. The original Golden Spike, however, is not at the park, but on display at Stanford University, not such an odd destination when one recalls that it was Governor Leland Stanford of California who helped drive the original.

A sentimental aside: Mary Ipsen was the only person in that crowd in 1942 who attended both the Driving and the Undriving of the Spike. She was a waitress on a mess car for the Promontory Mountain crew in May 1869.

TOP FOOD IN TOWN

Gearing up as an icon for the 1962 World's Fair, the Space Needle in Seattle, Washington, opened the previous year with the first revolving restaurant in the United States. It twirled 260 seats in a complete circle in one hour; the needle itself is a six-hundred-foot-high steel and glass tower. The popular Sky City restaurant still twirls and serves fine food in 360-degree splendor today.

A HISTORY OF WORLD'S FAIRS

Year	Venue	Name	Theme
1851	London	Great Exhibition of the Works of Industry of All Nations	
1853	New York		
1853	Dublin, Ireland		
1855	Paris	Exposition Universelle	
1862	London		
1867	Paris	Exposition Universelle	
1873	Vienna, Austria	Weltausstellung	
1874	Dublin, Ireland		
1876	Philadelphia	Centennial Exhibition	
1878	Paris	Exposition Universelle	
1884	New Orleans, Louisiana		
1885	Antwerp, Belgium		
1886	London		
1888	Melbourne, Australia		
1888	Glasgow, Scotland		
1889	Paris	Exposition Universelle	

Year	Venue	Name	Theme
1893	Chicago	World's Columbian Exhibition	
1894	San Francisco		
1895	Atlanta, Georgia		
1897	Brussels, Belgium		
1900	Paris	Exposition Universelle	
1901	Buffalo, New York	Pan-American Exposition	
1904	Saint Louis, Missouri	Louisiana Purchase Exposition	
1905	Liège, Belgium	Exposition Universelle et Internationale	
1906	Milan, Italy		
1907	Dublin, Ireland Hampton Roads, Virginia		
1909	Seattle, Washington		
1910	Brussels, Belgium		
1911	Turin, Italy		
1913	Ghent, Belgium		
1915	San Francisco	Panama-Pacific International Exposition	
1916	San Diego, California		

Year	Venue	Name	Theme
1922	Rio de Janiero, Brazil		
1924	Wembley, United Kingdom		
1925	Paris		
1926	Philadelphia		
1929	Barcelona, Spain		
1930	Seville, Spain		
1930	Antwerp, Belgium		
1930	Liège, Belgium		
1931	Paris		
1933	Chicago	Century of Progress International Exposition	
1935	Brussels, Belgium		
1937	Paris	Exposition Internationale	
1939	New York	New York World's Fair	The World of Tomorrow
1940	San Francisco	Golden Gate International Exposition	
1958	Brussels, Belgium	Expo '58	

Year	Venue	Name	Theme
1962	Seattle, Washington	Century 21 Exposition	Science
1964	New York	New York World's Fair	Peace Through Understanding
1967	Montreal, Canada	Expo '67	
1968	San Antonio, Texas	Hemisfair '68	The Confluence of Civilizations in the Americas
1970	Osaka, Japan	Expo '70	Progress and Harmony for Mankind
1974	Spokane, Washington	Expo '74	Celebrating a Fresh, New Environment
1975	Okinawa, Japan	Expo '75	The Sea We Would Like to See
1982	Knoxville, Tennessee	World's Fair	Energy Turns the World
1984	New Orleans, Louisiana	Louisiana World Exposition	The World of Rivers—Fresh Water as a Source of Life

Year	Venue	Name	Theme
1985	Tsukuba, Japan		Dwellings and Surroundings: Science and Technology for Man at Home
1986	Vancouver, Canada	World in Motion— World in Touch	
1988	Brisbane, Australia	World Expo '88	Leisure in the Age of Technology
1992	Seville, Spain	Expo '92	The Era of Discovery
1992	Genoa, Italy	Genoa Expo '92	Ships and the Sea
1993	Taejon, South Korea	Expo '93	The Challenges of a New Road to Development
1998	Lisbon, Portugal	Expo '98	The Oceans, a Heritage for the Future
2000	Hanover, Germany	Expo 2000	Man, Nature, and Technology

◆

The SHORTEST WAR in history was in 1896, when Zanzibar took on England for forty-five minutes . . . and lost.

WHO'S CALLING?

In 1878, the world's first telephone book was issued by the
New Haven, Connecticut, Telephone Company and
contained the names of the company's fifty subscribers.

CUCKOO: EVERY HOUR
ON THE HOUR

Around 1740, a certain German clock maker discovered how
to echo the cuckoo bird's sound with tiny twin bellows which
sent air through small pipes; he decided to make this
mellifluous tweet the sound his wall clocks would feature
instead of chimes, like everyone else's. As it became a sort of
art form, woodworkers began to add tiny details—cut gears,
painting, carved decorations and scenery—that made every
clock different. After the harsh indoor winters spent carving,
these clockmakers put their wares in sacks, put the sacks on
their backs, and took them down from the Alps to sell in the
villages. They were called *ührschleppers*.

A YEAR OF WEIRD HOLIDAYS

When you're looking for an excuse to celebrate, you can count
on somebody to pull through. Whether it's the United Nations
or a presidential proclamation, a day sponsored by a corporation
or registered by an individual with the Department of
Commerce (and a few that are just good-hearted nonsense),
every day's a holiday, as the following pages prove.

January

1	2	3	4	5	6	7
Z Day (Go first in line if your last name begins with Z)	Run It Up the Flagpole Day	Drinking Straw Day	Humiliation Day	Organize Your Home Day	Bean Day	Old Rock Day (Find one in your yard)
8	**9**	**10**	**11**	**12**	**13**	**14**
National Man Watcher's Day	Play God Day	Peculiar People Day (Say hello to one)	Rhubarb Day	National Pharmacist Day	Blame Someone Else Day	Dress Up Your Pet Day
15	**16**	**17**	**18**	**19**	**20**	**21**
Get to Know Your Customers Day	National Nothing Day	Judgment Day	Winnie-the-Pooh Day	Popcorn Day	Cheese Day	Squirrel Appreciation Day
22	**23**	**24**	**25**	**26**	**27**	**28**
National Blonde Brownie Day	Handwriting Day (Practice a lost art)	Eskimo Pie Patent Day	Broken Hearts Day	Bubble Wrap Appreciation Day	Thomas Crapper Day	Compliment Day
29	**30**	**31**				
National Puzzle Day	Fun at Work Day	Child Labor Day				

February

1	2	3	4	5	6	7
Robinson Crusoe Day	Groundhog Day	Dump Your Significant Jerk Day	Thank a Mailman Day	Weatherman's Day	Lame Duck Day	Charles Dickens Day
8	9	10	11	12	13	14
Kite Flying Day	Toothache Day	Umbrella Day	Satisfied Staying Single Day	Lost Penny Day	Get a Different Name Day	Ferris Wheel Day
15	16	17	18	19	20	21
Susan B. Anthony Day	Do a Grouch a Favor Day	My Way Day	National Battery Day	Chocolate Mint Day	Ember Tart Day	Love Your Pet Day
22	23	24	25	26	27	28
Be Humble Day	International Dog Biscuit Appreciation Day	Pancake Day	Samuel Colt's Pistol Patent Day	Pistachio Day	International Polar Bear Day	Floral Design Day
29						
Leap Day (every four years)						

March

1 Pig Day	**2** Old Stuff Day	**3** Stop the BS Day	**4** Holy Experiment Day (With thanks to William Penn)	**5** Multiple Personality Day (Try one on)	**6** Nothing Day	**7** Babysitters Safety Day
8 Be Nasty Day	**9** Panic Day (Don't)	**10** Barbie's Birthday	**11** Johnny Appleseed Day	**12** Middle Name Pride Day	**13** Jewel Day	**14** Potato Chip Day
15 Act Happy Day	**16** Lips Appreciation Day	**17** Submarine Day	**18** Forgive Mom and Dad Day	**19** Poultry Day	**20** Festival of ET Abduction Day	**21** Memory Day (Don't forget!)
22 Goof Off Day	**23** Chip and Dip Day	**24** Chocolate Covered Raisin Day	**25** Waffle and Pecan Day	**26** Make Your Own Holiday Day	**27** National "Joe" Day	**28** Something on a Stick Day
29 Festival of Smoke and Mirrors Day	**30** I Am in Control Day	**31** National Clams on the Half Shell Day				

April

1	2	3	4	5	6	7
International Tatting Day	National Peanut Butter and Jelly Day	Tweed Day	Check your Batteries Day	National Workplace Napping Day	Sorry Charlie Day (For all who've been rejected . . . and survived!)	No Housework Day
8	**9**	**10**	**11**	**12**	**13**	**14**
Vote Lawyers Out of Office Day	Name Yourself Day	Sibling Day	Eight Track Tape Day	Look Up at the Sky Day	Thank Your School Librarian Day	Pecan Day
15	**16**	**17**	**18**	**19**	**20**	**21**
Rubber Eraser Day	Stress Awareness Day	Cheeseball Day	Jugglers Day	Garlic Day	Look Alike Day (Dress like your favorite person)	Kindergarten Day
22	**23**	**24**	**25**	**26**	**27**	**28**
Jelly Bean Day	World Laboratory Animal Day	Pig in a Blanket Day	No Excuse Day	Hug an Australian Day	Tell a Story Day	Kiss Your Mate Day
29	**30**					
Shrimp Scampi Day	Hairstyle Appreciation Day					

May

1	2	3	4	5	6	7
Save the Rhinos Day	Robert's Rules of Order Day	Paranormal Day	Kite Day	National Hoagie Day	No Homework Day	International Tuba Day
8 Do Dah Day (Hats off to "Camptown Races")	**9** Lost Sock Memorial Day	**10** Clean Up Your Room Day	**11** Eat What You Want to Day	**12** Limerick Day	**13** Leprechaun Day	**14** Dance Like a Chicken Day
15 Chocolate Chip Day	**16** Wear Purple for Peace Day	**17** Pack Rat Day	**18** Youth Against Violence Day	**19** Frog Jumping Jubilee Day	**20** Eliza Doolittle Day	**21** National Waitress/Waiter Day
22 Buy a Musical Instrument Day	**23** Penny Day	**24** Ancestor Honor Day	**25** Tap Dance Day	**26** National Senior Health Day	**27** Body Painting Arts Festival	**28** Hamburger Day
29 End of Middle Ages Day	**30** My Bucket's Got a Hole in It Day (Hats off to square dancers)	**31** World No Tobacco Day				

June

1 Dare Day	**2** Rocky Road Day	**3** Repeat Day Repeat Day	**4** Hug Your Cat Day	**5** World Environment Day	**6** Teachers Day	**7** Chocolate Ice Cream Day
8 National Taco Day	**9** Donald Duck Day	**10** Yo-Yo Day	**11** Hug Holiday	**12** Machine Day (Plug it in)	**13** Race Unity Day	**14** Family History Day
15 Smile Power Day	**16** Hollering Contest Day	**17** Eat Your Vegetables Day	**18** Work at Home Fathers Day	**19** Sauntering Day	**20** Vegan World Day	**21** Baby Boomer's Recognition Day
22 Chocolate Éclair Day	**23** Let It Go Day	**24** Swim a Lap Day	**25** Take Your Dog to Work Day	**26** "Happy Birthday" to You Day	**27** Decide to Be Married Day	**28** Paul Bunyan Day
29 Camera Day (Snap something)	**30** Meteor Day (Hats off to Tunguska, Siberia, 1908)					

July

1	2	3	4	5	6	7
Canada Day	I Forgot Day	Compliment Your Mirror Day	Country Music Day	Workaholic Day	Take Your Webmaster to Lunch Day	Strawberry Sundae Day
8	9	10	11	12	13	14
Video Games Day	Lobster Carnival	Don't Step on a Bee Day	National Cheer Up the Lonely Day	Pecan Pie Day	Embrace Your Geekness Day	National Nude Day
15	16	17	18	19	20	21
Respect Canada Day	International Juggling Day	Cow Appreciation Day	Ice Cream Day	Get Out of the Dog House Day	Ugly Truck Contest Day	Tug of War Tournament
22	23	24	25	26	27	28
Rat Catchers Day (Hail to the Pied Piper!)	Vanilla Ice Cream Day	Virtual Love Day	Day Out of Time Day	All or Nothing Day	Take Your Houseplant for a Walk Day	Drive-Thru Appreciation Day
29	30	31				
Parents' Day	Mutts Day	All-American Soap Box Derby Day				

August

1	2	3	4	5	6	7
Friendship Day	National Ice Cream Sandwich Day	National Watermelon Day	Twins Day	National Mustard Day	Forgiveness Day	National Lighthouse Day
8	9	10	11	12	13	14
Sneak Some Zucchini onto Your Neighbor's Porch Night	National Polka Festival	National S'mores Day	Presidential Joke Day	Middle Child's Day	International Left-Handers Day	National Creamsicle Day
15	16	17	18	19	20	21
Relaxation Day	National Tell a Joke Day	National Thriftshop Day	Bad Poetry Day	Aviation Day	National Radio Day	Hawaii Day
22	23	24	25	26	27	28
Tooth Fairy Day	National Spongecake Day	Knife Day (First Bowie knife, 1838)	Kiss and Make Up Day	Women's Equality Day	Just Because Day	Race Your Mouse Day
29	30	31				
More Herbs, Less Salt Day	Toasted Marshmallow Day	National Trail Mix Day				

September

1	2	3	4	5	6	7
Emma M. Nutt Day (First female telephone operator)	National Blueberry Popsicle Day	Skyscraper Day	Newspaper Carrier Day	Be Late for Something Day	Read a Book Day	Neither Rain nor Snow Day
8	9	10	11	12	13	14
Pardon Day	Teddy Bear Day	Swap Ideas Day	No News Is Good News Day	National Pet Memorial Day	Defy Superstition Day	National Cream-Filled Donut Day
15	16	17	18	19	20	21
Make a Hat Day	Collect Rocks Day	Apple Dumpling Day	National Play-Doh Day	International Talk Like a Pirate Day	National Punch Day	International Peace Day
22	23	24	25	26	27	28
Elephant Appreciation Day	Checkers Day	Rabbit Day	National Comic Book Day	National Pancake Day	Crush a Can Day	Ask a Stupid Question Day
29	30					
Confucius Day	National Mud Pack Day					

October

1	2	3	4	5	6	7
World Vegetarian Day	Name Your Car Day	Techies Day	National Golf Day	Do Something Nice Day	Universal Children's Day	Bald and Free Day
8	**9**	**10**	**11**	**12**	**13**	**14**
Wallpaper Day	Moldy Cheese Day	National Angel Food Cake Day	Take Your Teddy Bear to Work Day	Farmer's Day	Navy Birthday	National Dessert Day
15	**16**	**17**	**18**	**19**	**20**	**21**
White Cane Safety Day	Dictionary Day	Wear Something Gaudy Day	No Beard Day	Evaluate Your Life Day	Brandied Fruit Day	Count Your Buttons Day
22	**23**	**24**	**25**	**26**	**27**	**28**
National Nut Day	TV Talk Show Host Day	National Bologna Day	Punk for a Day Day	Mule Day	Separation of Church and State Day	Plush Animal Lover's Day
29	**30**	**31**				
Hermit Day	National Candy Corn Day	National Magic Day				

November

1	2	3	4	5	6	7
National Authors' Day	Deviled Egg Day	Sandwich Day	King Tut Day	Guy Fawkes Day	Saxophone Day	Cook Something Bold Day
8	9	10	11	12	13	14
Dunce Day	Sadie Hawkins Day (First "girls get to ask" dance, 1938)	Forget-Me-Not Day	Air Your Dirty Laundry Day	National Pizza with the Works Except Anchovies Day	National Indian Pudding Day	Young Readers Day
15	16	17	18	19	20	21
Clean Your Refrigerator Day	Button Day	Take a Hike Day	Occult Day	Have a Bad Day Day	Absurdity Day	World Hello Day
22	23	24	25	26	27	28
Go for a Ride Day	You're Welcome Day	Use Even If Seal Is Broken Day	National Parfait Day	Buy Nothing Day	Pie in the Face Day	Red Planet Day
29	30					
Square Dance Day	Stay at Home Because You're Well Day					

December

1	2	3	4	5	6	7
Eat a Red Apple Day	Fritters Day	Roof Over Your Head Day	Wear Brown Shoes Day	Bathtub Day	National Gazpacho Day	Cotton Candy Day
8	9	10	11	12	13	14
Take It in the Ear Day	Pastry Day	Human Rights Day	National Noodle-Ring Day	Ding-a-Ling Day	Violin Day	Bouillabaisse Day
15	16	17	18	19	20	21
Bill of Rights Day	Chocolate-Covered Everything Day	Underdog Day	Roast Suckling Pig Day	Oatmeal Muffin Day	Games Day	Look at the Bright Side Day
22	23	24	25	26	27	28
Date Nut Bread Day	Roots Day	Eggnog Day	National Pumpkin Pie Day	Whiners Day	Fruitcake Day	Card Playing Day
29	30	31				
Tic-Tac-Toe Day	Festival of Enormous Changes Day	Unlucky Day				

THE SUMMER OF LOVE

If you were young and hip and peace was in your heart back in 1967, you wanted to head to San Francisco to celebrate the Summer of Love. But the summer of that year was actually the culmination of events and a way of life that had started long before. The "Summer of Love" was a phrase that meant a time, a feeling, a generation, a counterculture, when the hippie movement came to full fruition. It was the student dissatisfaction of U.S. involvement in Vietnam, civil rights, the murder of JFK, the discovery of LSD, the sexual revolution, and "Free Love," a time in which change was everything, and everything was possible. Youth was out to make the world a better place, and for a short time, everything seemed magical. By the end of 1967—just over the horizon—were political upheaval, the height of the Vietnam War, the Students for a Democratic Society, Kent State University, and more. The Summer of Love truly began long before 1967 . . . and it was the beginning of the end of a carefree time. Herewith a few stops on the road:

1963: LSD first appears on the street in sugar-cube form.

February 1965: The United States begins bombing Vietnam.

November 6, 1965: Appeal I, Bill Graham's first concert at the Fillmore in San Francisco, is held, featuring Jefferson Airplane and the Warlocks (soon to be the Grateful Dead).

December 4, 1965: The Grateful Dead perform their first show in San Jose, California.

1966: Timothy Leary founds the League of Spiritual Development, with LSD as the sacrament.

September 9, 1966: The first issue of the newspaper the *Oracle* appears on the streets of Haight-Ashbury, bringing word of the peace movement to the streets.

October 6, 1966: California outlaws the use of LSD.

November 5, 1966: Ten thousand people join the Walk for Love and Peace and Freedom in New York City.

1967: The original Council for the Summer of Love is created by the Family Dog, the Straight Theatre, the Diggers, the *Oracle*, and about twenty-five other individuals.

January 14, 1967: The Human Be-In in San Francisco's Golden Gate Park is attended by twenty thousand people. It is billed as the Gathering of the Tribes in a "union of love and activism," and is considered the beginning of the Summer of Love.

March 7, 1967: Alice B. Toklas dies.

March 26, 1967: The Be-In in New York's Central Park is held. Ten thousand people attend.

April 5, 1967: Grayline Bus starts "hippie tours" of Haight-Ashbury.

April 15, 1967: An anti–Vietnam War protest is held in New York, with four hundred thousand marchers.

May 1967: Paul McCartney announces that all the Beatles have "dropped acid."

May 19, 1967: The first U.S. air strike on Hanoi is made.

May 20, 1967: Flower Power Day is held in New York City.

June 2, 1967: The Beatles' *Sgt. Pepper's Lonely Hearts Club Band* is released.

June 16, 1967: The Monterey Pop Festival is held.

June 21, 1967: The Summer Solstice Party in Golden Gate Park is held.

July 1967: The Summer of Rioting takes place in the United States. Blacks take to the streets in Chicago, Brooklyn, Cleveland, and Baltimore.

July 24, 1967: Forty-three people die in Detroit—it is the worst rioting in U.S. history.

October 8, 1967: Che Guevara is killed in Bolivia by U.S.-trained troops.

October 21–22, 1967: Antiwar protesters storm the Pentagon.

December 1967: The Beatles release the *Magical Mystery Tour* album.

December 1967: The Stop the Draft movement is organized by forty antiwar groups; nationwide protests ensue.

December 5, 1967: One thousand antiwar protesters try to close a New York City induction center. Allen Ginsberg and Dr. Benjamin Spock are among the 585 arrested.

December 5, 1967: The Beatles open Apple Shop in London.

December 31, 1967: Abbie Hoffman, Jerry Rubin, Paul Krassner, Dick Gregory, and friends pronounce themselves "yippies."

Some Top 40 Hits During the Summer of 1967
"San Francisco (Be Sure to Wear Flowers in Your Hair),"
Scott McKenzie

"Let's Live for Today," Grass Roots

"Groovin'," Young Rascals

"Light My Fire," the Doors

"Society's Child (Baby I've Been Thinking)," Janis Ian

"White Rabbit," Jefferson Airplane

"A Whiter Shade of Pale," Procol Harum

"Somebody to Love," Jefferson Airplane

On the Summer of Love

We are here to make a better world.

No amount of rationalization or blaming can preempt the moment of choice each of us brings to our situation here on this planet. The lesson of the '60's is that people who cared enough to do right could change history.

We didn't end racism but we ended legal segregation.

We ended the idea that you could send half a million soldiers around the world to fight a war that people do not support.

We ended the idea that women are second-class citizens.

We made the environment an issue that couldn't be avoided.

The big battles that we won cannot be reversed. We were young, self-righteous, reckless, hypocritical, brave, silly, headstrong and scared half to death.

And we were right.

—ABBIE HOFFMAN (1936–1989), FORMER HIPPIE
AND POLITICAL ACTIVIST

◆

The word—or concept of—WHEN does not exist in the language of the Moken people, who are sea gypsies of the Andaman Sea living on the islands off the coast of Myanmar.

THOSE WERE THE DAYS
When the Dow Jones Industrial Average Hit Some Milestones

May 17, 1792: Buttonwood Agreement signed,
considered initial formation of NYSE
January 12, 1906: First close over 100
March 12, 1956: First close over 500
February 18, 1971: New York Stock Exchange, Inc.,
formed, a not-for-profit corporation
November 14, 1972: First close over 1,000
January 8, 1987: First close over 2,000
April 17, 1991: First close over 3,000
February 23, 1995: First close over 4,000
November 21, 1995: First close over 5,000
October 14, 1996: First close over 6,000
February 13, 1997: First close over 7,000
July 16, 1997: First close over 8,000
April 6, 1998: First close over 9,000
March 29, 1999: First close over 10,000
July 16, 1999: First close over 11,000

HIGHEST VOLUME DAY ON THE NEW YORK STOCK EXCHANGE
July 24, 2002: 2,812,918,977 shares traded

LOWEST NYSE VOLUME DAY
March 16, 1830: 31 shares traded

SOME NYSE TRADING FLOOR TECHNOLOGICAL FIRSTS
Ticker: 1867
Telephones: 1878
Electric lights: 1883
Automated quotation service: 1953

Radio pagers: 1966
Electronic ticker display boards: 1966
Designated Order Turnaround (DOT) system: 1976
Intermarket Trading System (ITS): 1978
Electronic display book: 1983
SuperDot 250: 1984
Integrated technology network: 1994–1996
Wireless data system: 1996

WE'RE HERE, WE'RE QUEER, GET USED TO IT

On June 27, 1969, a police raid at a gay bar called the
Stonewall Inn in New York City sparked nationwide
controversy and is considered the beginning of the modern
gay rights movement.

NEWS FLASH!!

One Times Square has enjoyed a long history as the flagship,
at least sentimentally, of New York City's Times Square. At
its completion in 1904 as the home of the *New York Times*, it
was the second-tallest building in New York City, at twenty-
five stories—and immediately became the site for New Year's
Eve celebrations. In 1907, the ball-dropping tradition began,
followed by more fame in 1928 when the moving headline
"zipper" became the most famous electronic billboard in the
world. In 1996, new owners found that the building would
best be put to use as a sign tower; the 12,048 lightbulbs were
changed to LED, and as of 2002, the completely tenantless
One Times Square was 99 percent covered in signage.

DECLARATIONS AND CONSTITUTIONALITY

John Hancock and Charles Thomson were the only two people who actually signed the Declaration of Independence on July 4, 1776. Most of the other forefathers signed on August 2, but the signature of Thomas McKean of Delaware did not appear on the printed copy that was authenticated on January 17, 1777. Some historians assert that he didn't affix his, shall we say, "John Hancock" until five years later, as he was serving in the army in 1776.

The United States Constitution is the oldest federal constitution in existence, ratified on June 21, 1788. The Bill of Rights, which codifies Amendments I through X of the Constitution, went into effect on December 15, 1791. At this writing there are twenty-seven amendments (including Amendment XXI, which repeals Amendment XVIII), the last enacted in 1992.

Constitutional Amendments
THE BILL OF RIGHTS (AMENDMENTS I–X)

Amendment I **Freedoms, Petitions, Assembly** (1791)
Freedom of religion, speech, the press, and right of petition

Amendment II **Right to Bear Arms** (1791)
Right of people to bear arms not to be infringed

Amendment III **Quartering of Soldiers** (1791)
No soldier shall be quartered in any house in times of peace without consent of the owner

Amendment IV **Search and Arrest** (1791)
Persons and houses to be secure from unreasonable searches and seizures

Amendment V **Rights in Criminal Cases** (1791)
In general, no person shall be held to answer for a capital crime, unless on a presentment or indictment of a grand jury

Amendment VI **Right to a Fair Trial** (1791)
Civil rights for a fair and speedy trial

Amendment VII **Rights in Civil Cases** (1791)
In civil cases, the right to trial by jury shall be preserved

Amendment VIII **Bail, Fines, Punishment** (1791)
Excessive bails, fines, and punishments prohibited

Amendment IX **Rights Retained by the People** (1791)
Constitutional rights shall not be construed to deny others retained by the people

Amendment X **States' Rights** (1791)
Powers not delegated are reserved by state or people

Amendment XI **Lawsuits Against States** (1795)
U.S. judicial power will not extend to suits against a state

Amendment XII **Presidential Elections** (1804)
Election of president and vice president; establishment of electoral college (*amended by Amendment XX*)

Amendment XIII **Abolition of Slavery** (1865)
Neither slavery nor involuntary servitude shall exist in the United States

Amendment XIV **Civil Rights** (1868)
Citizenship and its privileges; no state shall make or enforce any law which shall abridge the privileges or immunities of citizens, nor deprive any person of life, liberty, or property, without due process of law

Amendment XV **Black Suffrage** (1870)
Citizens' right to vote shall not be denied on account of race,
color, and previous condition of servitude

Amendment XVI **Income Taxes** (1913)
Congress has power to lay and collect taxes on incomes

Amendment XVII **Senatorial Elections** (1913)
Election, vacancies, and qualifications of U.S. senators

Amendment XVIII **Prohibition of Liquor** (1920)
(*repealed by Amendment XXI*)
No manufacture, sale, or transportation of intoxicating liquor

Amendment XIX **Women's Suffrage** (1920)
Citizen's right to vote cannot be denied on account of sex

Amendment XX **Terms of Office** (1933)
Terms for presidents, vice presidents, senators, and
representatives; filling the vacancy of office of the president

Amendment XXI **Repeal of Prohibition** (1933)
Repeal of Prohibition Amendment

Amendment XXII **Term Limits for the Presidency** (1951)
President may be elected to serve only two terms

Amendment XXIII **Washington, D.C., Suffrage** (1961)
Appointment of electors for the District of Columbia

Amendment XXIV **Abolition of Poll Taxes** (1964)
Citizens will not be denied the right to vote due to
failure to pay a poll tax or any other tax

Amendment XXV **Presidential Succession** (1967)
Succession of vice president to the presidency and
subsequent people in line

Amendment XXVI **18-year-old Suffrage** (1971)
Voting age is lowered from twenty-one to eighteen years of
age

Amendment XXVII **Congressional Pay Raises** (1992)
No congressional raises may take effect until there has been
an intervening election of representatives

The Failed Amendments

Many amendments have been proposed by Congress since the
ratification of the Constitution but have failed the second
step: acceptance by the states. The language of the bill
determines whether or not the amendment has an expiration
date by which it has to be passed; some are still outstanding
and pending ratification; others have expired.

ARTICLE 1 OF THE ORIGINAL BILL OF RIGHTS
(PROPOSED 1789; STILL OUTSTANDING)

This amendment, proposed in 1789, dealt with the number of
persons represented by each member of the House, and the
number of members of the House. It provided that once the
House had a hundred members, it should not have fewer than
a hundred, and once it reached two hundred, it should not
have fewer than two hundred. There are more than four
hundred members today. It was ratified by ten states, the last
in 1791.

THE ANTI-TITLE AMENDMENT
(PROPOSED 1810; STILL OUTSTANDING)

This amendment, submitted to the states in the 11th
Congress (in 1810), said that any citizen who accepted or
received any title of nobility from a foreign power, or who
accepted without the consent of Congress any gift from a

foreign power, would no longer be a citizen. Congressional research shows that the amendment was ratified by twelve states, the last being in 1812.

THE SLAVERY AMENDMENT
(PROPOSED 1861; STILL OUTSTANDING)

This amendment, also known as the Corwin Amendment, would prohibit Congress from making any law interfering with the domestic institutions of any state (slavery being specifically mentioned). It was proposed and sent to the states and is still outstanding. Congressional research shows that the amendment was ratified by two states, the last being in 1862.

THE CHILD LABOR AMENDMENT
(PROPOSED 1926; STILL OUTSTANDING)

In 1926, an amendment was proposed that granted Congress the power to regulate the labor of children under the age of eighteen. This amendment has been ratified by twenty-eight states; ratification by thirty-eight states is required for passage.

THE EQUAL RIGHTS AMENDMENT (ERA)
(PROPOSED 1972; EXPIRED UNRATIFIED, AFTER EXTENSION, 1982)

The ERA intended that equality of rights under the law not be denied on account of sex.

THE DISTRICT OF COLUMBIA VOTING RIGHTS AMENDMENT (PROPOSED 1978; EXPIRED UNRATIFIED 1985)

This amendment would have granted the citizens of Washington, D.C., the same full representation in Congress as any state.

UP, UP, AND AWAY

Versailles, France, September 19, 1783: A sheep,
a duck, and a rooster become the first passengers launched
in a hot-air balloon by a pair of French brothers, Joseph
and Ettienne Montgolfier.

Over Paris, November 21, 1783: The first recorded flight with
people (instead of livestock) soared for twenty-two minutes in
a paper and silk balloon, also built by the Montgolfiers.
Aboard were Pilatre de Rozier, who later became the first man
killed in an aircraft accident, and the Marquis d'Arlandes, an
infantry officer.

English Channel, 1785: French balloonist Jean-Pierre
Blanchard and American John Jeffries become the first to fly
across the English Channel, considered the first successful
trip in long-distance ballooning.

Ballooning in Wartime, 1794–1945: Right through the end of
World War II, balloons are used to survey, communicate, and
transport.

New Altitude Record Set, 1935: *Explorer II*, a helium gas
balloon with a pressurized chamber and two humans aboard,
sets the altitude record at 72,395 feet. The record was held for
twenty years.

Around the World, March 1–March 20, 1999: Swiss Bertrand
Piccard and Brian Jones of England left the Swiss Alps, and
nineteen days, one hour, and forty-nine minutes later, floating
over Mauritania, North Africa, became the first balloonists to
circumnavigate the globe without stopping or refueling.

COFFEE, TEA, OR VITAL SIGNS?

On May 15, 1930, Boeing hired Ellen Church, a nurse, to become the world's first airplane stewardess, flying on the Oakland-to-Chicago route. After being rejected for a position as a pilot, Church approached the airline with the idea that nurses on board commercial flights would allay civilians' fears and attract more passengers.

Stewardesses' careers in the 1930s were less than glamorous. Aside from the duties flight attendants perform today, they loaded luggage, made minor mechanical adjustments, fueled the planes, and even helped push them into the hangars. For this they earned $125 per month. The requirements, besides a nursing degree? Single, under 5 foot 4, and 115 pounds—and many of them were asked to promise to stay single for at least eighteen months.

OVER THE BOUNDING MAIN
Some of History's First Big Voyages

1304–1354:	Ibn Battuta sails to India and China.
1405–1433:	Cheng Ho voyages to Africa and Indonesia.
1419:	Portuguese explorers begin to sail along the west coast of Africa.
1492:	Columbus sails to America.
1497:	Vasco da Gama sails around Africa to reach India.
1519–1522:	Magellan's ship sails around the world (Magellan not so lucky).
1577–1580:	Francis Drake sails around the world.
1642:	Tasman sails to Australia.
1768–1779:	Captain Cook explores the Pacific.

THE MORE-OR-LESS HUNDRED YEARS WAR

The Hundred Years War was an episodic struggle between France and England and actually lasted 116 years—from 1337 to 1453. It began when King Philip VI of France attempted to confiscate the English territories in the duchy of Aquitaine, and ended when the French finally expelled the English from the continent, except for Calais. Much of the time there was no conflict at all: truces and uneasy peace alternated with sudden raids, plundering, and naval battles.

WHAT TH' . . . ?

The first speech bubble is thought to have been drawn by Richard Fenton Outcalt for his comic strip "The Yellow Kid" in 1896.

ALL THAT JAZZ

In about 1895, a group of seven- to twelve-year-old boys in New Orleans got together and formed what some experts call the original jazz band. They advertised themselves as the Razzy Dazzy Spasm Band and, later, the Razzy Dazzy Jazzy Band. It's thought that the word "jazz" originally meant fornication, and it was said, "If the truth was really known about the origins of Jazz, it would certainly never be mentioned in polite society."

◆

The world's oldest continuous LEGISLATIVE BODY is Iceland's official parliament; called the Althingi, it was established in 930 in Iceland by Viking-era settlers.

GREAT MOMENTS IN PIZZA

Since ancient times, flat bread was cooked on a hot stone—and sometimes dates, honey, and olive oil were added. Some food historians say that this was the beginning of pizza, and that the word itself is from an old Italian word meaning "point." But there were thousands of years and many culinary advancements before pizza—as we know it today—came to the table, including the import of the tomato to Italy from Peru in 1522. Throughout the seventeenth and eighteenth centuries, bakers in Naples continued to serve a local dish of bread with tomatoes mixed in, but it wasn't until 1889 that an entrepreneuring Neapolitan concocted the pizza we currently enjoy . . .

1889: Raffaele Esposito created a dish for visiting King Umberto of Italy and his consort, Queen Margherita. In order to impress them, he prepared three kinds of pizza: one with pork fat, cheese, and basil; one with garlic, oil, and tomatoes; and another with mozzarella, basil, and tomatoes—known even today as Margherita pizza.

1905: Naples immigrant Gennaro Lombardi opened the first U.S. Pizzeria in New York City at 53½ Spring Street.

1948: The first commercial pizza-pie mix, Roman Pizza Mix, was produced in Worcester, Massachusetts, by Frank A. Fiorello.

1953: Dean Martin sang, "When the moon hits your eye like a big pizza pie, that's amore."

1957: Frozen pizzas were introduced and found in local grocery stores. The first was marketed by Celentano Brothers. Pizza soon became—and still remains—the most popular of all frozen foods.

A HOLIDAY IN THE MAKING
A Few Things About Turkey Day

Popular history tells us the Pilgrims landed on December 11, 1620 (no Thanksgiving this year).
The first Thanksgiving feast that the Pilgrims hosted, in 1621, lasted three days.
The first time all thirteen original colonies celebrated Thanksgiving together was in 1777.

VACANCY

In 1925, the first motel—the Motel Inn—opened in San Luis Obispo, California. The word "motel" was coined by the architect Arthur Heineman, and just so travelers wouldn't be confused, a neon sign alternately flashed the words "Hotel" and "Mo-tel" so that motorists would know that both their bodies and their automobiles were welcome.

TICK-TOCK

The first version of the sundial appeared somewhere between 5000 and 3500 BCE. It consisted of a stick or pillar placed vertically; the length of the shadow determined the time of day. Though there are certainly new variations of the sundial—analog, and digital, to name a few—they are essentially the same: a gnomon "shadow-maker" and a dial face, dependent on the sun rising every day.

◆

In 1908, AIRPLANE ADVERTISING, via a banner towed behind the plane, was used for the first time, to promote a Broadway play.

WHEN EMILY POST SPEAKS...

In 1922, people listened when *Etiquette* was first published. Today, Miss Emily Post would surely be horrified with cell phones, e-vites, young ladies with pierced belly buttons, and scores of other undreamt social sins. Herewith a few tips on manners, from back when they meant something:

When to Shake Hands
When gentlemen are introduced to each other they always shake hands.

When a gentleman is introduced to a lady, she sometimes offers her hand—especially if he is someone she has long heard about from friends in common, but to an entire stranger she generally merely bows her head slightly and says, "How do you do!"

What to Say When Introduced
The correct formal greeting is always: "How do you do?"

There are a few expressions possible under other circumstances and upon other occasions. If you have, through friends in common, long heard of a certain lady, or gentleman, and you know that she, or he, also has heard much of you, you may say when you are introduced, "I am very glad to meet you," or "I am delighted to meet you at last!" Do not use the expression "pleased to meet you" then or on any occasion. And you must not say you are delighted unless you have reason to be sure that she, or he, also is delighted to meet you.

When Dinner Is Announced
It is the duty of the butler to "count heads" so that he may know when all the company has arrived. As soon as he has announced the last person, he notifies the cook. The cook being ready, the butler, having glanced into the dining room to

see that windows have been closed and the candles on the table lighted, enters the drawing room, approaches the hostess, bows, and says quietly, "Dinner is served."

Dressing When the Income Is Limited

No one can dress well on nothing a year; that must be granted at the outset. But a woman who has talent, taste, and ingenuity can be suitably and charmingly dressed on little a year, especially at present.

First of all, to mind wearing a dress many times because it indicates a small bank account is to exhibit a false notion of the values in life. Anyone who thinks well or ill of her, in accordance with her income, cannot be too quickly got rid of! But worthwhile people are influenced in her disfavor when she has clothes in number and quality out of proportion to her known financial situation.

It is tiresome everlastingly to wear black, but nothing is so serviceable, nothing so unrecognizable; nothing looks so well on every occasion.

YOU ARE GETTING SLEEPY . . .

At latitude 25° north, the longest day is longer than the longest night, and the shortest day is longer than the shortest night:

Longest Day	13h 42m
Longest Night	13h 25m
Shortest Day	10h 35m
Shortest Night	10h 18m

◆

TITANIC (the 1997 movie) takes forty minutes longer to watch than it took *Titanic* (the ship) to sink.

WONDERS OF THE WORLD LISTS

Since ancient times, people have put together many "seven wonders" lists. The first list is usually attributed to Antipater of Sidon, who listed the structures in a poem around 140 BCE:

> I have set eyes on the wall of lofty Babylon
> on which is a road for chariots,
> and the statue of Zeus by the Alpheus,
> and the hanging gardens,
> and the Colossus of the Sun,
> and the huge labour of the high pyramids,
> and the vast tomb of Mausolus;
> but when I saw the house of Artemis that mounted to the
> clouds, those other marvels lost their brilliancy, and I said,
> "Lo, apart from Olympus, the Sun never looked
> on aught so grand."
> —Antipater, Greek Anthology 9.58

SEVEN WONDERS OF THE ANCIENT WORLD
2680 BCE: The Pyramids of Egypt
600 BCE: The Hanging Gardens of Babylon
550 BCE: The Temple of Artemis (Diana) at Ephesus
ca. 450 BCE: The Statue of Zeus (Jupiter) at Olympia
350 BCE: The Mausoleum at Halicarnassus
280 BCE: The Colossus at Rhodes
Third century BCE: The Pharos (Lighthouse) of Alexandria

With the passage of time, several other lists began to appear, none credited to an author as was the original. Herewith some of the more popular:

THE SEVEN WONDERS OF THE MEDIEVAL MIND
ca. 200 BCE: Stonehenge (England)
70–80 CE: The Colosseum (Rome, Italy)
First century CE: The Catacombs of Kom el Shoqafa
(Alexandria, Egypt)
221–206 BCE and present state **1368–1644:**
The Great Wall of China
Fifteenth century CE: The Porcelain Tower of Nanjing (China)
537 CE: The Hagia Sophia (Constantinople)
1173–1370 CE: The Leaning Tower of Pisa (Italy)

THE SEVEN WONDERS OF THE MODERN WORLD
1930: The Empire State Building (New York City)
1975–1991: The Itaipú Dam (Brazil/Paraguay)
1973: The CN Tower (Toronto, Canada)
1880–1914: The Panama Canal (Panama)
1994: The Channel Tunnel (England/France)
1923: The North Sea Protection Works (Netherlands)
1937: The Golden Gate Bridge (San Francisco, California)

THE SEVEN FORGOTTEN MODERN WONDERS OF THE WORLD
1858: The Clock Tower/Big Ben (London, England)
1889: The Eiffel Tower (Paris, France)
1965: The Gateway Arch (St. Louis, Missouri)
1960: The Aswan High Dam (Egypt)
1935: Hoover Dam (Arizona/Nevada)
1927–1941: Mount Rushmore National Memorial (South
Dakota)
1998: The Petronas Towers (Kuala Lumpur, Malaysia)

THE SEVEN FORGOTTEN WONDERS OF THE MEDIEVAL MIND
1279–1223 BCE: Abu Simbel Temple (Egypt)
1113–1152 CE: Angkor Wat (Cambodia)

1630 CE: Taj Mahal (India)
1023 CE: Mont Saint-Michel (Normandy, France)
100–1650 CE: The Moai Statues/Easter Island (Rapa Nui, Chile)
447–432 BCE: The Parthenon (Athens, Greece)
Unknown: The Shwedagon Pagoda (Myanmar)

THE FORGOTTEN WONDERS
1350 CE: The Aztec Temple (Mexico City, Mexico)
Several centuries BCE: The Banaue Rice Terraces (The Philippines)
750–842 CE: The Borobudur Temple (Indonesia)
1500 CE: The Inca City (Machu Piccu, Peru)
700 CE: The Mayan Temples of Tikal (Northern Guatemala)
100 BCE: The Temple of the Inscriptions (Palenque, Mexico)
550 BCE: The Throne Hall of Persepolis (Iran)
Fourth century BCE: The rock-carved city of Petra (Jordan)
1859–1867: The Suez Canal (Egypt)
1973: The Sydney Opera House (Australia)
1638–1648: The Red Fort in India (Agra)

◆

TRUE OR FALSE?

How does a polygraph know when you're lying? The test simultaneously monitors several of the suspect's physiological functions—breathing, pulse, and galvanic skin response—and prints them on graph paper. The results show when the greatest biological responses occur, which indicate stress and, consequently, lying.

◆

Tropical RAINFORESTS are the world's oldest ecosystems.

GOOD TIMES, BAD TIMES

The theory of biorhythms states that one can determine the physical, emotional, intellectual—and some now say spiritual—cycles that forecast the patterns of a person's critical days and periods of high and low energy. Biorhythms change the behavior or physiology of an organism, which are maintained and generated by a biological clock. The four types of rhythms, which rarely intersect at once, and can greatly affect a person's demeanor and performance are:

Intellectual cycle (32 days)	Affects memory, ability to study, mental activities, clearness of thoughts
Emotional cycle (27 days)	Affects feelings, mood, emotions, and state of mind, as well as sensibility to the surrounding world and to other people
Physical cycle (22 days)	Controls physical and sexual activity, body coordination, resistance to illnesses, and endurance
Intuitive (or spiritual) cycle (37 days)	Controls perception of beauty, creative inspiration, and the reception or apprehension of subconscious impulses, that is, intuition itself; also called spiritual rhythm

◆

Before 1933, the DIME was legal as payment only in transactions of $10 or less. In that year, Congress made the dime legal tender for all transactions.

GREAT MOMENTS IN INVENTING

6500 BCE: Potter's wheel
4000 BCE: Cosmetics (Egypt)
2000 BCE: Toilet flush, Minoan civilization (Crete)
1500 BCE: Scissors (Egypt)
100 BCE: Roller bearing (France or Germany)
1268: Eyeglasses, Salvino D'Armate (Italy)
1540: Artificial limbs, Ambrose Paré (France)
1589: Hosiery-knitting machine, Rev. William Lee (England)
1564: Pencil (England)
1756: Mayonnaise (France)
1816: Phosphorus match, François Derosne (France)
1830: Lawn mower, Edwin Budding, John Ferrabee (England)
1846: Sewing machine, Elias Howe (United States)
1848: Chewing gum, John Curtis (United States)
1849: Bullet, Claude Minie (France)
1849: Safety pin, Walter Hunt (United States)
1853: Condensed milk, Gail Borden (United States)
1859: Oil well, Edwin L. Drake (United States)
1862: Machine gun, Richard J. Gatling (United States)
1866: Lip reading, Alexander Melville Bell (United States)
1877: Concrete, Joseph Monier (France)
1886: Coca-Cola, Dr. John Stith Pemberton (United States)
1891: Zipper, W. L. Judson (United States)
1897: Worm gear, Frederick W. Lanchester (England)
1899: Aspirin, Dr. Felix Hoffman (Germany)
1899: Tape recorder, Valdemar Poulsen (Denmark)
1909: IUD (intrauterine device), R. Richter (Germany)
1910: Airplane autopilot, Elmer A. Sperry (United States)
1926: Aerosol can, Erik Rotheim (Norway)
1929: Scotch tape, Richard Drew (United States)
1933: Cat's eye road reflector, Percy Shaw (England)

1938: Ballpoint pen, Lazlo Biro (Argentina)
1943: Aqualung, Jacques-Yves Cousteau and Emile Gagnan (France)
1945: Tupperware, Earl W. Tupper (United States)
1947: Holograph, Dennis Gabor (England)
1951: Oral contraceptive, Gregory Pincus, Min Chuch Chang, John Rock, Carl Djerassi (United States)
1957: Pacemaker, Clarence W. Lillehie, Earl Bakk (United States)
1972: Prozac, Bryan B. Malloy (Scotland), Klaus K. Schmiegel (United States)
1972: Compact disk, RCA (United States)
1972: Video disk, Philips Company (Netherlands)
1972: Electronic mail, Ray Tomlinson (United States)

◆

LONG LIFE

A Few of Earth's Longest-Living Animals and Plants and Their Recorded Maximum Ages:

giant tortoise: 200 years
human: 122 years
sturgeon: 100 years
blue whale and golden eagle: 80 years
African elephant: 77 years
Amborella: 140 million years
King's Holly (*Lomatia tasmanica*): 43,000 years
creosote plants (*Larrea divaricata*): 11,700 years
bristlecone pine (*Pinus longaeva*): 4,000–5,000 years

◆

A FEMTOSECOND is one quadrillionth of a second, or one millionth of a nanosecond.

"MAZEL TOV—IT'S A BOY!"

Jewish circumcision, *bris milah*, has no meaning when performed before the eighth day of life because kabbalistic writings teach that the child has to transcend the physical— the seven days of creation—to the metaphysical before a covenant joining body and soul can occur.

DOES IT ALL ADD UP?

Though the earliest mention of an abacus is in 190 CE in a Chinese book, *Supplementary Notes on the Art of Figures*, many historians suggest that a Roman version of what might be called the world's first computer preceded the Eastern version. Travel on the Silk Road brought not only social and scientific innovation but commerce, and very likely the introduction of this counting board.

Another view suggests that there is no connection at all between the Roman and Chinese abaci, and that their appearances are the result of convergent evolution—the process by which different and unrelated individuals reached the obvious solution for improving the original adding machine: counting on five fingers while using the fingers of the other hand for place holders.

NICKEL-AND-DIME THEM

Frank Woolworth opened his first five-and-dime store in 1879. A fixture in American downtowns throughout the first half of the twentieth century, Woolworth's was the first store to put its merchandise out for the customers themselves to touch, select, and purchase.

THE FRUIT OF THEIR LABOR

Steven Jobs and Steve Wozniak made nearly as big a splash with their 1984 Apple computer as the serpent did in the Garden of Eden. It changed the world—and yet the specifications below for its debut version are almost laughably inadequate today:

Name: Macintosh
Manufacturer: Apple
Type: Home computer
Origin: United States
Year: January 1984
End of production: October 1, 1985
Keyboard: Full-stroke 59-key
CPU: Motorola MC 68000
Speed: 7.83 MHz
RAM: 128 KB (expandable to 512 KB)
ROM: 64 KB
Text modes: 40 characters x 32 lines bitmapped pseudo-
    character mode
Graphic modes: 512 x 342 dots
Colors: black-and-white 9-inch monitor
Sound: 4 voices, 12-octave sound @ 22 kHz
Size/Weight: 13.6 inches (H) x 9.6 inches (W) x 10.9
    inches (D)/16.5 pounds
I/O ports: Two serial (RS 232/422) for printer and modem,
    mouse, external floppy drive, sound out
Built-in media: One 400K 3.5-inch internal floppy drive;
    400K external drive optional
OS: Macintosh System 1.0
Power supply: Built-in power supply unit
Price: $2,495 (United States, 1984); £1,795 (United
    Kingdom, 1984)

THE HISTORY OF THE BICYCLE

It seems unimaginable that it took more than five thousand years for man to progress from the invention of the wheel to the bicycle. A short history of a great ride . . .

3500 BCE

The wheel was invented.

1490

Artist, architect, and master inventor Leonardo da Vinci may have sketched an astonishing facsimile of a modern-day bicycle, which apparently never got any further than the drawing board.

c. 1790—The Célérifère

There are reports that Count Mede de Sivrac designed and was seen riding the *célérifère*, a type of rolling machine with two in-line wheels connected by a wooden beam, much more like a hobby horse than anything else. The rider moved by pushing along with his or her feet, as on a scooter.

1817—The Walking Machine

Baron Karl Drais von Sauerbronn improved on de Sivrac's invention by adding an important innovation: steering. His new mode of transportation, which he devised for his own use to get around the royal gardens, allowed the rider to point the front wheel in the direction he or she wanted to go. Unfortunately, the entire machine was made of wood, which made for a rather unsettling ride.

1860s—Pedals and Cranks

Historians say that the father-and-son team of Pierre and Ernest Michaux, French carriage makers, invented the bicycle sometime in the 1860s, citing the younger Michaux as "the father of the bicycle"; though others disagree and insist that the invention was some years earlier, it is agreed that Ernest added the modern pedal and cranks in 1864—and a brand-new means of propulsion.

1865—The Velocipede

The "fast-foot" was also a two-wheeler . . . but this time with the pedals attached directly to the front wheel. Fast (or faster, anyway) it may have been, but it was also commonly known as "the boneshaker." It was made entirely of wood.

1870—The High-Wheel Bicycle

This is the version associated with the Gay Nineties—men with bowler hats and handlebar mustaches riding head and shoulders above the street traffic—and it is the first version of the bicycle to be made entirely of metal. Previous to this time, metallurgy was not advanced enough to make small, light parts. Hard rubber tires were also added for the first time, affording the rider a much smoother ride. Manufacturers made the radii of the wheel as long as the rider's leg would allow—they had by now realized that the larger the wheel, the further a rider could travel with just one rotation of the pedal.

1871—The Penny Farthing

Engineer James Starley's "ordinary" or "penny farthing" was the first really efficient bicycle, consisting of a small rear wheel and large front wheel pivoting on a simple tubular frame, with tires of rubber.

1880—The High-Wheel Tricycle

Basically, this version was built like the two-wheeler, but the extra wheel made it easy for women in skirts and corsets to balance their cycle alongside those of their male friends.

1880s—The High-Wheel Safety

In one of many new design improvements, a smaller wheel was used in the front in an attempt to prevent tipping over.

1885—The Hard-Tired Safety Bicycle

This version marked a return to the version with two equal-sized wheels, but with a great advancement: metal was now easy enough to work with that a chain and sprocket could be added, so that every turn of the pedal gave the rider both speed and distance.

1888—The Pneumatic-Tired Safety

A Scotsman, John Dunlop, developed the pneumatic to give his son a more comfortable ride on his tricycle. With this cheaper, more comfortable, and now safe version of the bicycle, manufacturers clamored to get in on what had finally made its way beyond a fad.

1899—"Saddle Bags"

The African American inventor Jerry M. Certain patented a parcel carrier for bicycles. It straddled both sides of the wheel, affording the rider two places to stow gear.

1920s–1950s—Kids' Bikes

After World War I, bicycles for children became big sellers, and manufacturers such as Sears, Roebuck and Montgomery Ward, and later Schwinn resized bikes for smaller bodies and added glamorous automobile and motorcycle blandishments, such as chrome and stripes.

1950s–1970s—Three-Speed Bikes

The elegant English bicycles such as Raleigh, on which riders could change gears for the first time, eased topographical challenges.

1970s–1980s—Ten-Speed Bikes

The ten-speed derailleur bike became popular in the 1970s, as both racing and long-distance riding for pleasure became sporting sensations. Though the derailleur had been invented several decades before in Europe, the standard for American bicycles was the "fixed-and-free" gear system, where the hub was threaded for a free wheel on one side and a fixed gear on the other.

1980s–present

Riders took the sport one step further, and mountain bikes joined the rest of the worldwide "extreme sports" boom. Ironically, the construction of today's mountain bikes hearkens back to the Schwinns of the late 1930s, with fore-wheel brakes, cantilever frames, and spring-fork suspension.

"NO BRAIN, NO PAIN"

Scientists now believe that lobsters, crabs, and other creatures without backbones do not feel a thing when popped into a pot of boiling water.

"THE EAGLE HAS LANDED . . ."

At exactly 4:17:40 P.M., Eastern Daylight Time, on July 20, 1969, *Apollo 11* landed on the surface of the moon. That, of course, is Earth time . . . but will we ever know what time it was on the moon?

◆

On Thursday, August 14, 1941, the last EXECUTION in the Tower of London took place. Josef Jakobs, a German spy, was shot by an eight-man firing squad.

HOW DOES YOUR BABY GROW?

The sheer fascination of watching a child in infancy can distract the casual observer from seeing that a child's growth—physical, social, mental, and lingual—proceeds on an extremely smooth schedule (though for parents it may not seem so). A brief look at baby's first months:

First Month
Can recognize parents' voices
Can see objects up to 10 inches away
Oohs and ahhs

Second Month
Begins to understand that crying gets attention
Exhibits emotions
Holds head up for short periods

Third Month
Begins vowel sounds
Discovers hands and feet
Recognizes peoples' scents

Fourth Month
Explores by testing
Laughs hard when tickled
Can bear weight on legs

Fifth Month
Begins to show decision-making behavior
Transfers objects from hand to hand
Recognizes own name

Sixth through Ninth Month

Begins to respond to his or her name
Learns to reach with accuracy
Uses thumb and fingers to pick up
Understands that an object might be behind something
Learns to mimic

Tenth through Twelfth Month

Feels pride when praised
Builds and disassembles
Waves good-bye
Indicates wants with gestures
May learn to scribble

Thirteenth through Fifteenth Month

Plays peekaboo
Eats with fingers
Walks backward
Can identify body parts by pointing
Can draw a line

Sixteenth through Eighteenth Month

Turns pages of a book
Enjoys pretend games
Responds to directions
Can speak in phrases

◆

None of the BRONTË sisters—Anne, Charlotte, or Emily—
lived until their fortieth birthday.

A BRIEF ACCOUNT OF
MODERN GAY HISTORY

1533: King Henry VIII began the English common-law tradition of sodomy laws.

1792: France decriminalized sexual acts between men.

1825: Karl Heinrich Ulrichs (d. 1895), considered by many to be the world's first gay activist, was born. He dared to say that homosexuals were natural—not sinners, diseased, or criminal. In 2002, Italian publisher Roberto Massari dedicated a new wine, Rosso Gayardo, to him.

1836: The last known execution for homosexuality in Britain took place.

1869: The term *homosexuality* appeared in print for the first time in a German pamphlet written by Károly Mária Kertbeny (1824–1882), an Austrian-born Hungarian journalist, memoirist, and human rights campaigner. Kertbeny's thesis emphasized that the state should have no part to play in the policing of private sexual behavior. Kertbeny claimed himself to be a "Normalsexualer."

1871: Paragraph 175 (known formally as §175 StGB; also known as Section 175, in English) was a provision of the German criminal code from May 15, 1871, to March 10, 1994. It made homosexual acts between males a crime, and in early revisions the provision also criminalized bestiality.

1892: The word *bisexual* is first used in its current sense in Charles Gilbert Chaddock's translation of Richard von Krafft-Ebing's *Psychopathia Sexualis*.

1897: Sex researcher Magnus Hirschfeld (1868–1935) founded the Scientific Humanitarian Committee to organize for gay rights and the repeal of Paragraph 175.

1903: In New York City, police conducted the first recorded raid on a gay bathhouse, the Ariston on West Fifty-fifth Street. Seven men received sentences ranging from four to twenty years in prison.

1906: The first homosexual periodical, *Der Eigene* ("The Special One"), was published in Germany. Until it ceased publication in 1931, it had an average of fifteen hundred readers per issue.

1908: San Francisco city officials closed the Dash, the city's earliest known gay bar. It was located at 574 Pacific Street, and also offered drag shows.

1910: Anarchist Emma Goldman first began speaking publicly in favor of gay rights.

1924: The Society for Human Rights in Chicago became the earliest known gay rights organization in the United States. Founder Henry Gerber modeled his organization on the homosexual rights movement in Germany.

1937: The pink triangle was first used to identify homosexual prisoners in Nazi concentration camps.

1945: Prisoners interned for homosexuality were not freed from Nazi camps but required to serve out the full term of their sentences under Paragraph 175.

1948: Alfred Kinsey published *Sexual Behavior in the Human Male*, revealing to the public that homosexuality is far more widespread than was commonly believed.

1950: The Mattachine Society, the first openly gay organization in the United States, was founded in Los Angeles by Henry Hay (d. 2002 at the age of ninety) and others, all of whom were associated with the American Communist Party. They were soon ousted in favor of more politically conservative leaders.

1955: The Daughters of Bilitis, a pioneering national lesbian organization, was founded.

1964: *Life* magazine published a path-breaking feature article, "Homosexuality in America."

1969: Patrons at the Stonewall Inn, a gay bar in New York's Greenwich Village, fought back during a police raid, sparking a three-day riot. The widespread protest that ensued is considered the beginning of the modern gay rights movement.

1970: The first gay pride parade in the United States was held in New York City.

1973: The American Psychiatric Association removed homosexuality from its official list of mental disorders.

1974: Kathy Kozachenko became the first openly gay or lesbian American elected to public office, when she won a seat on the Ann Arbor, Michigan, city council.

1977: Anita Bryant led a successful crusade against a Miami gay rights law.

1978: Gay men in the United States and Sweden—and heterosexuals in Tanzania and Haiti—began showing signs of what would later be called AIDS.

1979: On October 14, one hundred thousand gays, lesbians, bisexuals, and straight supporters marched on Washington, D.C., celebrating gay pride and demanding equal rights for homosexuals under the law.

1981: The Moral Majority started its antigay crusade.

Writer Vito Russo published *The Celluloid Closet*, in which he outed and decoded homosexuality in the movies.

Alan P. Bell led a Kinsey study that suggested that homosexuals are born with that predisposition and not influenced by traumatic experiences during childhood.

1982: The term AIDS, for acquired immune deficiency syndrome, was used for the first time. In the United States 853 deaths had been reported. An answering machine in the home of a volunteer for the newly formed Gay Men's Health Crisis, Rodger McFarlane, was the world's first AIDS hotline. It received more than one hundred calls the first night. McFarlane later became the first paid director of the Gay Men's Health Crisis.

1989: The Danish parliament allowed legal marriage among homosexuals.

1993: The World Health Organization removed homosexuality from its list of diseases.

President Bill Clinton instituted the "Don't Ask, Don't Tell" policy for the U.S. military, permitting gays to serve in the military but banning them from any homosexual activity. This policy led to the discharge of thousands of men and women from the armed forces.

1994: Paragraph 175, the 1871 German law criminalizing sex between males, was repealed after the country's reunification.

1996: American gay activists were dealt a double disappointment when the U.S. Senate voted against same-sex marriage with the Defense of Marriage Act; it also rejected a bill that barred job discrimination against gays.

1999: Russell Henderson pleaded guilty to kidnapping and felony murder in the 1998 death of Matthew Shepard, a gay college student, in Laramie, Wyoming.

The Vermont Supreme Court ruled that homosexual couples were entitled to the same benefits and protections as wedded heterosexual couples.

2000: The Vermont legislature approved civil unions.

2003: The U.S. Supreme Court ruled in *Lawrence v. Texas* that sodomy laws in the United States are unconstitutional. Justice Anthony Kennedy wrote, "Liberty presumes an autonomy of self that includes freedom of thought, belief, expression, and certain intimate conduct."

2004: Same-sex marriages became legal in Massachusetts.

HOW LONG?
When "When?" is a complex word:

Semidiurnal . . . . twice a day
Diurnal . . . . daily
Semiweekly . . . . twice a week
Weekly . . . . once a week
Biweekly . . . . every 2 weeks
Triweekly . . . . every 3 weeks
Bimonthly . . . . every 2 months
Trimonthly . . . . every 3 months
Biannual . . . . twice a year
Semiannual . . . . every 6 months

Annual	every year
Perennial	year after year
Biennial	2 years
Triennial	3 years
Quadrennial	4 years
Quinquennial	5 years
Sexennial	6 years
Septennial	7 years
Octennial	8 years
Novennial	9 years
Decennial	10 years
Undecennial	11 years
Duodecennial	12 years
Quindecennial	15 years
Vigennial	20 years
Tricennial	30 years
Semicentennial	50 years
Demisesquicentennial	75 years
Centennial	100 years
Quasquicentennial	125 years
Sesquicentennial	150 years
Terquasquicentennial	175 years
Bicentennial	200 years
Tercentennial or tricentennial	300 years
Quadricentennial	400 years
Quincentennial	500 years
Sexacentennial	600 years
Septuacentennial	700 years
Octocentennial	800 years
Nonacentennial	900 years
Millennial	1,000 years
Bimillennial	2,000 years

A PARTIAL HISTORY OF
GLORIOUS FOOD

*From the ground to the shelves, the origins, discoveries, and
introductions of some of life's greatest gustatory pleasures:*

(BCE)	
17,000	Grain
10,000	Almonds
9000	Sheep
8000	Apples and lentils
7000	Pork
7000	Beans
6500	Cattle domestication
6000	Wine
6000	Cheese
6000	Maize
5500	Honey
5000	Olives and olive oil
5000	Potatoes
5000	Milk
4000	Grapes
4000	Citrus fruits
3600	Popcorn
3200	Chicken domestication
3000	Butter
3000	Onions, garlic, and spices
2700	Tea
1500	Chocolate
1200	Sugar
1000	Pickles
500	Sausages
490	Pasta

(CE)	
62	Ice cream
2nd century	Sushi
3rd century	Lemons
220	Tofu
7th century	Spinach
9th century	Coffee
9th century	Cod
15th century	Breton and Portuguese fishermen fish off New England
1484	Hot dogs
16th century	Americans begin to export local foods to other continents
1588	Potato arrives in Ireland
1592	Pot luck
17th century	Doughnuts in America
1610	Bagel invented in Poland
1621	Pilgrims host first Thanksgiving
1654	Kosher food introduced in United States
18th century	French fries
1708	Casseroles
1756	Mayonnaise
1762	The Earl of Sandwich invents his eponymous foodstuff
1767	Soda water
1767	Franciscan brothers introduce grapes and vineyards to California
1773	Boston Tea Party
1784	Lollipops
1789	Thomas Jefferson's pasta machine
1794	United States Navy serves up first rations
1811	McIntosh apples

1825	Jean Anthelme Brillat Savarin declares: "Tell me what you eat and I will tell you who you are."
1826	Fondue
1830s	Hopping John
1845	Poland Spring water
1847	Chinese food introduced in America
1853	Potato (or Saratoga) chip
1856	Condensed milk
1867	Synthetic baby food
1868	Fleischmann's Yeast
1869	Campbell's Soup
1869	Thomas Adams invents chewing gum
1876	Heinz Ketchup
1880s	Railroad car dining introduced
1886	Coca-Cola
1891	Quaker Oats
1893	Chili served at the Chicago World's Fair
1894	Hershey bar
1897	Jell-O
1897	Sears & Roebuck prints world's first brownie recipe
1902	Horn & Hardart's Automats
1903	Canned tuna
1904	Ice cream cone
1906	United States: federal pure food and drug law passed
1911	Crisco
1912	First self-service grocery stores open
1915	Kraft processed cheeses
1919	Prohibition begins in the United States
1920	Good Humor Bars
1920	La Choy chinese foods

1921	Wonder Bread
1923	Sanka
1927	Kool-Aid
1927	Oscar Mayer packaged sliced bacon
1928	Twinkie
1929	Clarence Birdseye sells first frozen foods
1930	Wonder Bread sells first sliced bread
1931	Tacos in United States
1931	*The Joy of Cooking* first printed
1933	Waldorf salad invented
1935	Pan Am introduces airline food
1936	First Howard Johnson's opens
1937	First shopping cart
1938	Canned soda
1939	U.S. government offers food stamps
1941	M&Ms
1941	Garbage disposals
1945	Tupperware
1946	Culinary Institute of America opens
1947	Aluminum foil
1949	Electric dishwasher
1953	Welch's Howdy Doody glasses
1957	Tang
1962	Instant mashed potatoes
1963	Julia Child's *The French Chef* appears on TV
1964	Buffalo wings
1965	Gatorade
1991	Salsa outsells ketchup as top condiment in United States
1992	USDA replaces The Four Basic Food Groups with the Food Pyramid

AMERICAN FURNITURE PERIODS

Though a distinct European style accompanied Americans in their furniture design and construction when they crossed the Atlantic in the early seventeenth century, the citizens of the New World soon developed a freer, less constraining style of their own that mirrored their views of living.

Jacobean (1603–1690): English style, medieval in appearance, ornate carvings, and a dark finish; retained many Elizabethan characteristics, but ornamentation became less prominent

Early American (1640–1700): Rudimentary furniture constructed from local woods modeled after European, mostly Jacobean, furniture; mostly oak and pine

William and Mary (1690–1725): After William and Mary of England (r. 1689–1694), often characterized by ball feet and padded or caned seats; Dutch and Chinese influences

Queen Anne (1700–1755): A graceful refinement of William and Mary style; characterized by cabriole and fiddleback chair back.

Colonial (1700–1780): Combined characteristics of William and Mary, Queen Anne, and Chippendale; more conservative than its contemporary European counterparts

Georgian (1714–1760): Named after George I and George II, who ruled England from 1714 to 1760; a more ornate version of Queen Anne; often gilded

Pennsylvania Dutch (1720–1830): A simple, utilitarian country style with Germanic influences; often painted

Chippendale (1750–1790): Named after British cabinet maker Thomas Chippendale; more elaborate development of Queen Anne furniture

Robert Adam (1760–1795): Named for architect Robert Adam, who studied ancient architecture in Italy; reproduced by cabinetmakers in South Carolina; classically designed pieces to match his classically designed homes

Hepplewhite (1765–1800): Named after English designer and cabinetmaker George Hepplewhite; neoclassic and delicate, featuring contrasting veneers and inlays

Federal (1780–1820): Combination of the neoclassic furniture style characteristics of both Hepplewhite and Sheraton; light construction, graceful legs, delicate lines throughout

Sheraton (1780–1820): Named for English designer Thomas Sheraton, the most popular style of the Federal period; a neoclassical style characterized by delicate straight lines, light construction, contrasting veneers, and neoclassical motifs and ornamentation

Duncan Phyfe (1795–1848): Considered by many experts and art historians to be an adaptation of Adam, Sheraton, Hepplewhite, and American Empire rather than a style unto itself

American Empire (1800–1840): A dark, classical style akin to French Empire; closely carved with moderate proportions

Shaker (1820–1860): A utilitarian style produced by the religious group in self-contained communities; characterized by straight tapered legs and woven chair seats

Victorian (1840–1910): Named for Queen Victoria of England, a return to gothic form, heavy proportions, and dark, elaborate ornamentation; the first mass-produced furniture

Arts and Craft (1880–1910): Simple, straight, flat utilitarian design; also referred to as mission furniture

Art Nouveau (1890–1910): A naturalistic style characterized by intricately detailed patterns and flowing, curving lines

Scandinavian Contemporary (1930–1950): A simple, utilitarian design style in natural wood, popularized by Danish and Swedish designers

◆

IT'S SPUTNIK!

The space age began on October 4, 1957, with the launch of a Soviet artificial satellite. Named *Sputnik*, a Russian word for "traveling companion of the world," it was the size of a basketball and weighed only 183 pounds—yet it circled Earth every ninety-eight minutes. It carried a thermometer and two radio transmitters and worked for twenty-one days.

CAN YOU HEAR ME NOW?

While we credit Alexander Graham Bell with the telephone, others contributed the groundwork.

In the nineteenth century, Charles Boursel suggested that a diaphragm making/breaking contact with an electrode might be used to transmit sound electrically. Johann Philipp Reis followed up in 1861 with a device consisting of a metallic strip and vibrating membrane that broke an electrical circuit to transmit a simple tone. In the 1870s Elisha Gray used a set of reeds tuned to different frequencies to induce currents in electric coils as a variation on harmonic telegraphy.

On June 3, 1875, Alexander Graham Bell and Thomas Watson succeeded in transmitting what they called speech-like sounds using electrically connected vibrating membranes. Bell received the patent for his device in 1876.

NATIONAL HOLIDAYS AROUND THE WORLD

There's always something to celebrate somewhere…

Afghanistan:	August 19
Albania:	November 28
Algeria:	November 1
Andorra:	September 8
Angola:	November 11
Antigua and Barbuda:	November 1
Argentina:	May 25
Armenia:	September 21
Australia:	January 26
Austria:	October 26
Azerbaijan:	May 28
Bahamas:	July 10
Bahrain:	December 16
Bangladesh:	March 26
Barbados:	November 30
Belarus:	July 3
Belgium:	July 21
Belize:	September 21
Benin:	August 1
Bhutan:	December 17
Bolivia:	August 6
Bosnia and Herzegovina:	November 25
Botswana:	September 30
Brazil:	September 7
Brunei:	February 23
Bulgaria:	March 3
Burkina Faso:	December 11
Burundi:	July 1

Cambodia:	November 9
Cameroon:	May 20
Canada:	July 1
Cape Verde:	July 5
Central African Republic:	December 1
Chad:	August 11
Chile:	September 18
China, People's Republic of:	October 1
Colombia:	July 20
Comoros:	July 6
Congo:	August 15
Congo, Democratic Republic of:	June 30
Costa Rica:	September 15
Côte d'Ivoire:	August 7
Croatia:	October 8
Cuba:	December 10
Cyprus:	October 1
Czech Republic:	October 28
Denmark:	June 5
Djibouti:	June 27
Dominica:	November 3
Dominican Republic:	February 27
East Timor:	November 28
Ecuador:	August 10
Egypt:	July 23
El Salvador:	September 15
Equatorial Guinea:	October 12
Eritrea:	May 24
Estonia:	February 24
Ethiopia:	May 28
Fiji:	2nd Mon. of October
Finland:	December 6
France:	July 14

Gabon:	March 12
Gambia:	February 18
Georgia:	May 26
Germany:	October 3
Ghana:	March 6
Greece:	March 25
Grenada:	February 7
Guatemala:	September 15
Guinea:	October 2
Guinea Bissau:	September 24
Guyana:	February 23
Haiti:	January 1
Honduras:	September 15
Hungary:	August 20
Iceland:	June 17
India:	January 26
Indonesia:	August 7
Iran:	April 1
Ireland:	March 17
Israel:	April or May*
Italy:	June 2
Jamaica:	August 6
Japan:	December 23
Jordan:	May 25
Kazakhstan:	December 16
Kenya:	December 12
Kiribati:	July 12
Korea (North):	September 9
Korea (South):	August 15
Kuwait:	February 25
Kyrgyzstan:	August 31
Laos:	December 2

*Variable holiday, falling on a different date each year.

Latvia:	November 18
Lebanon:	November 22
Lesotho:	October 4
Liberia:	July 26
Libya:	September 1
Liechtenstein:	August 15
Lithuania:	February 16
Luxembourg:	June 23
Macedonia:	August 2
Madagascar:	June 26
Malawi:	July 6
Malaysia:	August 31
Maldives:	July 26
Mali:	September 22
Malta:	September 21
Marshall Islands:	May 1
Mauritania:	November 28
Mauritius:	March 12
Mexico:	September 16
Micronesia, Federated States of:	May 10
Moldova:	August 27
Monaco:	November 19
Mongolia:	July 11
Morocco:	July 30
Mozambique:	June 25
Myanmar (Burma):	January 4
Namibia:	March 21
Nauru:	January 31
Nepal:	July 7
Netherlands:	April 30
New Zealand:	February 6
Nicaragua:	September 15
Niger:	December 18

Nigeria:	October 1
Norway:	May 17
Oman:	November 18
Pakistan:	March 23
Palau:	July 9
Panama:	November 3
Papua New Guinea:	September 16
Paraguay:	May 14–15
Peru:	July 28
Philippines:	June 12
Poland:	May 3
Portugal:	June 10
Qatar:	September 3
Romania:	December 1
Russia:	June 12
Rwanda:	July 1
St. Kitts and Nevis:	September 19
St. Lucia:	February 22
St. Vincent and the Grenadines:	October 27
Samoa:	June 1
San Marino:	September 3
São Tomé and Príncipe:	July 12
Saudi Arabia:	September 23
Senegal:	April 4
Serbia and Montenegro:	April 27
Seychelles:	June 18
Sierra Leone:	April 27
Singapore:	August 9
Slovakia:	September 1
Slovenia:	June 25
Solomon Islands:	July 7
Somalia:	July 1
South Africa:	April 27

Spain:	October 12
Sri Lanka:	February 4
Sudan:	January 1
Suriname:	November 25
Swaziland:	September 6
Sweden:	June 6
Switzerland:	August 1
Syria:	April 17
Taiwan:	October 10
Tajikistan:	September 9
Tanzania:	April 26
Thailand:	December 5
Togo:	April 27
Tonga:	June 4
Trinidad and Tobago:	August 31
Tunisia:	March 20
Turkey:	October 29
Turkmenistan:	October 27
Tuvalu:	October 1
Uganda:	October 9
Ukraine:	August 24
United Arab Emirates:	December 2
United States:	July 4
Uruguay:	August 25
Uzbekistan:	September 1
Vanuatu:	July 30
Vatican:	April 24
Venezuela:	July 5
Vietnam:	September 2
Yemen:	May 22
Zambia:	October 24
Zimbabwe:	April 18

(source: *CIA World Factbook*)